LIVING PROOF

HOW LOVE DEFIED GENETIC LEGACY

TIFFANY GRAHAM CHARKOSKY

Published by Little A, New York
www.apub.com

Amazon, the Amazon logo, and Little A are trademarks of Amazon.com, Inc., or its affiliates.

EU product safety contact:
Amazon Media EU S. à r.l.
38, avenue John F. Kennedy, L-1855 Luxembourg
amazonpublishing-gpsr@amazon.com

ISBN-13: 9781662532207 (hardcover)
ISBN-13: 9781662532214 (paperback)
ISBN-13: 9781662532191 (digital)

Cover design by Zoe Norvell
Cover image: Composure, by Erin Cone (2009) © Erin Cone,
© Elnur / Shutterstock

Printed in the United States of America

First edition

PRAISE FOR *LIVING PROOF*

"A relatable, honest, poignant look into motherhood, love, and overcoming. Inspiring and hopeful. Loved it!"

—Zibby Owens, host of *Totally Booked with Zibby*

"Toggling between the losses of childhood and adulthood, Charkosky sets out to write about illness and death, but *Living Proof* is a testament to the power of courage, hope, and love. Above all, love. I read this heartbreaking but life-affirming book in one sitting, rooting for every character."

—Thrity Umrigar, bestselling author of *The Space Between Us* and *Honor*

"Tiffany Graham Charkosky writes a beautiful, compelling narrative about motherhood, death, and grief from the perspective of a woman whose health is too risky for 'even a ridiculously expensive' life insurance option, a woman who lived 'the paradox of being a healthy person who is treated like a sick person,' a woman for whom surgery is preventive medicine. But it is the incredible way that she writes about love intertwined with forgiveness that creates a memoir worth returning to again and again."

—Brandi Larsen, cowriter of *Uncultured*

"*Living Proof* documents the grief, the growth, and the courage behind one woman's decision to investigate her genetic legacy. In this honest, unflinching memoir, Tiffany Graham Charkosky shares a deeply personal story that is at times wrenching but ultimately empowering—one that shows it is possible to rewrite the future."

—Laura Maylene Walter, author of *Body of Stars*

"Tiffany Graham Charkosky draws a shimmering narrative line across generations, from the mother she lost to the children she fears leaving. In the minimally charted land of genetic testing, this book acts as a bold, unflinching, and ultimately heartening travelogue."

—Cheryl E. Klein, author of *Crybaby* and senior editor at *MUTHA Magazine*

"Vivid and heartrending, *Living Proof* is the moving account of a woman facing the impossible circumstance of being a brand-new mother while facing down the limits of her body. Open and raw, Tiffany shares the story of facing a diagnosis straight on, ultimately showing us how to be brave, generous, and—finally—forgiving to herself and the body she was born into. This memoir was impossible to put down."

—Margaret Kimball, author of *And Now I Spill the Family Secrets*

"'This is a love letter,' Tiffany Graham Charkosky writes, overthrowing all expectations of what a memoir of genetic disorder can be. In *Living Proof*, Charkosky weaves a profoundly moving story of connection, hope, and all the ways legacy unfolds backward and forward through time. While Charkosky's story is sparked by Lynch syndrome, she taps into the deepest truth of life—we are infinitely connected to everyone who came before us and everyone who will come after. For anyone who has lost a parent or become one, who has forged a future with a partner (or dreams to), who has tried to heal their past while staying present, this story is for you."

—Cait Weiss Orcutt, author of *Valleyspeak*

"*Living Proof* is a moving and beautifully written—masterfully constructed—memoir. It is also a gripping, almost terrifying journey, during which Tiffany Graham Charkosky is forced to travel from the comforting world of a loving family and rewarding career into the mysteries of genetic predestination. Once I started reading this tale, I couldn't put it down. It's so brave, so important. An amazing achievement I'm certain readers will cherish."

—David Lynn, editor emeritus of *The Kenyon Review*

LIVING PROOF

For my mom

AUTHOR'S NOTE

At every step along the journey of this story, I found myself wishing for something to make me feel less alone. Less alone in my thoughts, my fears, and my feelings. Once the idea to write this book took hold, it wouldn't let me go. I hope to offer a window into the experience of genetic testing and the different ways I felt its impact over time, and that in doing so, I can help someone else—maybe you, maybe someone you love—feel seen.

While the events in this book are true to my memory, I understand that no two people experience the same thing in the same way. Some names have been altered to protect the privacy of the individuals involved.

The decisions I describe in this book were made in consultation with my medical team and family. They are not intended as medical advice or recommendations for others.

PART ONE

OCTOBER 2011

The Call

For most of my life, I viewed my mom's death when I was eleven as simply bad luck—terrible luck, yes, but something I had survived. Her death was a lump of clay I had shaped into a useful part of my character, a source of wisdom, and, most importantly, something firmly in the past. It was old luck that no longer had any bearing on me.

This belief shattered on a night in October, eighteen years after her funeral, with a phone call from my dad.

He never called just to check in, so when I saw DAD flash across my screen, I held it up to my husband, excused myself from the table, and stepped into a quieter spot. The living room seemed calm compared to the dinner chaos behind me. From there, I could still hear the clatter of my son's bowl hitting the hardwood floor, followed by our dog pouncing on its remnants. My dad's voice, too loud in the phone yet somehow muffled by static, broke through.

"I have some information from your Aunt Mary."

The phone grew heavy in my hand, and the nerves in my arms electrified. "What kind of information?" I asked.

"Your Uncle Jeff had some type of testing done right before he died. Mary sent me a letter from his doctor and said she was leaving it up to me to decide if I wanted to share it with you kids." He wasn't calling to ask if I wanted to know what the letter said. He was processing the existence of this letter. I was his oldest, so he called me first. He was trying to figure out if I was also his last call, or what he'd say to my brother and sister after we hung up.

When it came to information about myself, even remotely related, I couldn't help but seek it out. If I thought about starting a garden, I checked out a half dozen books from the library. When I was pregnant, I read obsessively about child development, labor, epidurals, baby names, cloth diapers, breastfeeding, immunizations, car seats, formula, parenting styles, day care options. When the ultrasound technician asked if we wanted to know the baby's sex, there was no question—of course we wanted to know.

But my dad's pinched voice carried a warning: Once I knew what he was about to share, I could never unknow it. I lowered myself to the floor, crossed my legs, and traced my fingers over the row of books on my shelf. I drew a heart in the dust.

My husband, Brian, came around the corner. "Everything okay?" he mouthed silently.

I shook my head and closed my eyes.

"Of course I need you to tell me," I said to my dad. My teeth chattered, though I wasn't cold. "Isn't calling me basically saying you have something I need to know?"

As my dad spoke, I learned there was a reason my mom died when she was thirty, and her brother at forty-six. The reason was still bad luck, but it wasn't a random strike of lightning. It was genetic bad luck. Bad luck my siblings and I each had a 50 percent chance of having inherited ourselves. If I was a carrier, there was a 50 percent chance I had already passed it on to my two-and-a-half-year-old son, Ben. The reason was called Lynch syndrome, and based on genetics, family history, and mathematics, it was nearly certain my mom died because of it.

After hanging up, I met Brian in the bathroom to help with Ben's bath. I poured tepid water over the bubbles in his hair and remembered my mom doing the same with my brother and me as we squished into the tub together. Her death, my grief, and the years of sickness preceding it flashed through my mind like images on a filmstrip gone haywire. I saw her skeletal face and felt my inability to help her. A familiar mixture of fear, anger, and guilt stirred back to life.

I let Ben play in the tub until his fingers wrinkled. I toweled him off and powdered his belly. I told him a story about a boy named Wren who had a flying bike and a pack of adoring friends, and lay next to him long after he fell asleep. When I shuffled into my own room, I wondered if I felt our house shifting on its foundation or if the damage was happening inside me. Would I become a whisper inside my son, a screaming void, a shadow figure visiting his dreams, a voice he forgets, an extinction in his ecosystem?

Had I already passed this on, our genetic heritage, a dormant volcano disguised as a mountain, waiting?

1991

Before

I was nine years old, sitting on the edge of our yellow porcelain bathtub as my mom brushed mascara onto her eyelashes. One brown eye appeared larger at first, off balance for a moment, until she did the other and her face became familiar again. She had freckles all over, just like me. With practiced fingers, she wove her auburn hair into a French braid. I had red hair too, though a lighter strawberry blond, and my eyes were green, like my dad's. Once she was done with her hair, she braided mine and added a ribbon.

She was younger than the other moms, and so pretty it hurt my pride to look at her sometimes. Her fingers were long and thin, unlike my stubby ones with chewed nails. I wore my jean skirt and the matching denim shirt that day, with folded-over ruffled socks and white Keds. She made sure my outfits were always clean and put together, my hair braided or crimped or curled. The night before, my mom had sat with me at the dining room table long past my bedtime while I finished the outline I'd forgotten I needed for a report on Wisconsin. I'd wept and hiccuped my way through. She didn't let me off the hook, but she didn't leave me alone downstairs either.

I sat with her this morning in my silent, self-prescribed penance. My seven-year-old brother, Danny, bounced into the bathroom wearing a bow tie and suspenders with his jeans, trying to imitate the kid from the movie *Problem Child.* He rummaged through the cupboard for hair spray to slick back his hair. Our brindle boxer came in too, upright on her hind legs, coaxed forward with a piece of cheese by our little sister, Brittany, who wore one of our dad's Bruce Springsteen T-shirts. My mom laughed at all of us: Danny for his obsession with that ridiculous movie, Brittany for being a ragamuffin, and me for keeping her up all night.

Fragments of an essay by Erma Bombeck hung on the living room wall called "I've Always Loved You Best Because . . ." There was a picture of each of us above the description of why that child was the mother's favorite. I was the oldest, the "first miracle." Danny was the middle, the one who went "to bed with dirty feet." Brittany was "the Baby" with the empty baby book. She bought this framed piece at a craft fair, and I can still remember her hammering the nails for it into the wall, giddy over her good fortune in finding something that described her life so perfectly.

My mom's fingers never rested. She stenciled a pattern around the border of our living room. She stripped a century of paint from the wood trim and covered the walls with cross-stitch pieces. She always had a sewing project, either to hang on our walls or to give as gifts. I can still picture her holding her embroidery hoop over her crossed legs while her friends drank coffee on our porch. She made me a quilt for my eighth birthday, not minding as I wandered the craft store, touching each of the dozens of floral fabrics she chose and would later pin together in perfect squares.

At the kitchen table, we dredged cubes of pork in flour before shoving them onto wooden sticks and dipped chicken into milk and crushed cornflakes. Together, we pinched closed the kolacky my mom learned to make from my Grandma Graham so my dad could enjoy his favorite cookies every Christmas.

Before she got sick, our house pulsed with the energy of childhood—scabby knees, screams and taunts, never-ending games played with kids who drifted in and out of the neighborhood like stray cats. Something was always unfair. Alliances formed and crumbled as quickly as sandcastles.

Some of these kids belonged to our mom's friends, ladies who spooned powdered coffee into mugs at the dining room table. Others were kids my mom babysat for extra money to justify her days at home with us. When we moved onto Rosewood Avenue in 1986, the garage doors still had glass windows. After too many foul balls hit off our baseball tee shattered the panes, my dad replaced them with plywood, painting it light gray to match the house.

My dad cemented a metal swing set, complete with monkey bars, a trapeze, rings, and a slide, between our garage and the neighbor's. I loved the feeling of flipping over on the rings and performing routines from the top of the monkey bars, the moment of suspension, an instant of fear, pulling myself back up, triumphant. Sometimes, my hands slipped away and I fell onto the muddy grass, knocking the wind from my chest, my fear stretching out until I regained my breath. More than once, dark blue half-moons formed under my eyes, a sharp contrast to my pale, freckled skin. "Raccoon eyes," my dad called them, never worried I wouldn't bounce right back up.

In fourth grade, my teacher passed out awards to our class. I yearned for the coveted "Best Handwriting" or "Teacher's Pet" certificate. Instead, I was named "Most Optimistic." At the time, this felt like a throwaway award, something given to someone who didn't excel at the more noteworthy categories. But when I brought it home, my mom's delight transformed it into a badge of honor.

I was born a couple of months after my mom turned nineteen. My dad was twenty-one. I knew I was an accident, but they never made me feel like one. If anything, it was the opposite. Every year on Christmas Eve, they made a mountain of homemade egg rolls and egg foo yong and other Americanized versions of Chinese food and had all their friends and family over for a party that started after Midnight Mass. I fell asleep by the Christmas tree to the sounds of laughter and woke up every Christmas morning with a letter from Santa written in unfamiliar handwriting. They went through the same fanfare on my birthday one week later, never correcting my assumption that the ball falling on Times Square or the pots and pans banging in the streets outside were for anything other than me.

OCTOBER 2011

The Snake

Ben hunched over his red Spider-Man shoes, insistent on fastening the Velcro strips himself. My son's wispy blond hair hung over his face, but I didn't need to see his eyes to know how focused he was. Once finished, he jumped up and looked back toward the floor, checking to make sure the lights in his heels still glowed. He'd already outgrown a pair of the exact same shoes, and these were beginning to look tight too.

Satisfied, Ben turned to me and asked, "What would your mom be to me?"

He asked variations of this question all the time, trying to piece together the world he knew with the old photo albums he liked to look at before bed. Ben loved pointing out every person in every picture, matching the shaggy, carefree versions of his relatives to the grown-ups they'd become. He wasn't usually interested in talking about the people he'd never met, but I always named them anyway.

"Your Grandma Julie would be like Grandma Suzie, except my mom instead of Dad's," I said. After staring at my bedroom ceiling most of the night before, with my dad's news overshadowing all my other thoughts, his question this morning unsettled me, like he was inside my mind.

Ben stopped bouncing from one red, blinking foot to the other. "As nice as her?"

I didn't know if anyone could be as nice to Ben as my mother-in-law, but I still said, "Yes, of course she'd be as nice. She'd love you just as much."

"As much?"

"At least as much." It seemed like all her friends would have called my mom their best friend, and each of her children believed we were her favorite. I knew she would have carved out a singular space in her heart for her only grandchild. "You'd love her too."

Ben scrunched his nose and gave this some thought. "Maybe."

It was impossible for me to tell, all these years later, if she really was as sunny as I remembered her, or if I had polished her to perfection in her absence.

As the sun shone through the windows smudged with nose prints and fingerprints, illuminating the dog hairs along the floorboards and crumbs sticking to the table, I checked to make sure Ben's day care bag had the extra underwear and outfit he needed, just in case. I removed the artwork from the day before, suddenly feeling guilty that I worked instead of staying home to make crafts with him. I wiped the table clean.

Ben ran in a circle around our downstairs, through the living room, dining room, and kitchen, his shoes flickering with every step. Our chocolate Lab, Buckeye, joined him. One moment, he was screaming in laughter, and the next, he tripped over his own foot and crashed face-first into the doorjamb. I was right there, but still too far away to stop him.

Ben howled, holding his hand up to his eye. I knelt down to see his eyebrow already swelling around a dent pressed into the delicate sand-colored hairs. I grabbed a bag of frozen blueberries, pulled him onto my lap, and held them to his hot, wet face. After several minutes, once his cries turned to sniffles, I peeked beneath the bag. His skin was intact, but taut like an overfilled balloon.

"Are you more scared or more hurt?" I asked, trying to gauge what he needed.

Ben answered by rekindling his cries.

I checked the time. I was late, again. Ben pressed his face into my chest, and as I cupped the back of his head into my palm, he grew quiet, softening into me. I couldn't remember the last time I'd been held like this, when the mere presence of my mom could make me feel better. But I closed my eyes and there it was, the feeling that lived inside me like a snake, always ready to rise silently from the ether and wrap itself around me, almost suffocating: I still wanted my mom.

1991–1992

The Eclipse

We were driving home to Ohio from Myrtle Beach when the first hint of her illness struck.

My mom curled up, a beaten dog moaning, arms crossed over her stomach and eyes squeezed shut. She pulled her knees tight to her chest, rocking herself across the back seat. I'd never seen her, or anyone, in pain like this. I'd certainly never felt it. When it wasn't our turn to occupy her empty seat up front, Danny, Brittany, or I were trapped beneath her and next to her, crying and trying to console our mom and each other, all at the same time. Our dad seemed scared in a way I'd never seen. He squeezed the steering wheel so tight I thought it would snap in half, and kept yelling at all of us that it was just sun poisoning. Even to my nine-year-old ears, I heard him trying to make us believe something he didn't believe himself as we all barreled down the freeway toward some god-awful fate. She cried for the entire drive home.

I didn't know pain like this could come from inside someone's body, gripping so tightly they didn't care who witnessed it or what they sounded like. It was like she was possessed by a demon that preyed on mothers, making their children invisible and burning unforgettable images into their minds. I wanted to be home but was terrified at the thought of the engine stopping and uncovering the source of those screams.

For nearly a year, my mom's pain drove her to the hospital. Each time, she was sent home, undiagnosed. I eavesdropped on whispered conversations between my parents, with my grandma, and my mom talking to her sister or her friends. What I heard was that the doctors didn't know what was wrong. They scanned her ovaries and uterus and found nothing. She was twenty-eight. She was healthy. She was young. This was in her head. She worked too hard, first going to nursing school when Brittany was a baby and studying all night, then passing her nursing boards and taking overnight shifts at the hospital. She took on too much and needed a break. The message I kept hearing was that whatever this was, she was doing it to herself.

Nobody said this, but what I grew to believe was that we, her children, had made her sick. We were too much work for her. Not knowing what was wrong changed the climate in our house. Our laughter was replaced by the constant feeling of impending doom. I became afraid to ask my mom for anything, of doing something wrong, making her worse, of having any needs at all. Even on the days she seemed normal, I stopped trusting her, waiting for whatever was wrong to happen again.

One morning before school, after our mom had been to the hospital more than twenty times, Danny, Brittany, and I sat around our wooden kitchen table, slurping sugary milk from our cereal bowls. Standing against the stove in his gray mechanic's pants, arms crossed over his chest, my dad told us our mom was having exploratory surgery that day.

"Does she have cancer?" Danny asked.

"Danny!" I shrieked, making his name louder at the end, Dan-NEEE! I must have said his name like that a million times throughout our childhoods, all in preparation for this moment when he took the fears I wouldn't name and gave them a word. We all knew what cancer was, having seen our mom's dad, Grandpa Mitchell, battle it for years. Our grandma on our dad's side had died from it a few years earlier too. They both appeared so old and sick it seemed impossible for our mom to have the same disease—and equally impossible that whatever she had wasn't just as bad.

"Don't say that." My dad's lips flattened into a straight line, and he put his hands inside his pockets. Even in the mornings when his pants were fresh from the dryer, I loved how they still smelled like oil from the auto body shop.

Clouds kept moving over the sunlight streaming through the lacy kitchen curtains. One second, there was a shadow pattern on the wall, and the next, there was nothing. I couldn't have known that this morning would demarcate all the uncertain days that came before her diagnosis from every single one that came after.

~

A sick mother changes the entire biome of her family, with everyone around her adapting in their own ways to a new environment. Almost two years passed between that car ride and actually losing her. The part that seems the cruelest is that my memories of her sickness have eclipsed most of my memories of her life. Each day, as tiny pieces of the mother I knew were erased, our home became a forest I no longer knew my way around.

~

The Cleveland Great American Rib Cook-Off took place against the shimmering backdrop of Lake Erie and the city skyline. The air was thick with the scents of smoky meat and sweaty bodies rising from the steaming asphalt. Charred ears of corn sizzled on grills, and local cover bands played on a stage, their music blasting through speakers into the mob of people. My favorite food was the homemade chips, made by sticking whole potatoes onto a mechanical spiral blade that dumped the thin slices into hot oil.

We parked only a few short blocks away, in a free spot my dad had discovered years before. Finding it open felt like a day's worth of good luck. My dad unfolded the wheelchair that lived in our car now.

My mom wrapped her arms around his neck as he bent over to lift her from the front seat. The skin covering her calf muscles hung from her shinbones like laundry on a line. I wondered how her legs would ever be strong again. Going out in public with my mom was so much work, but today she seemed happy, and that made it worth pretending this was normal. Her wheelchair seemed to hit every crack and bump in the sidewalk. By the time we walked through the gate, it seemed impossible that we were supposed to be on a fun family outing. I felt every eye of the large crowd on my family. My mom perched in her wheelchair, and all I could see was her birdlike skeleton and charcoal eyes protruding from her chalky-white skin.

She saw the shame and fear on my face before I realized I was staring. "You're embarrassed to be seen with me?" She spit out these words in a voice I didn't recognize. I had ruined one of her increasingly rare good days.

She wasn't my mother in these moments.

And yet.

When my friends wanted to host a surprise birthday party for our friend Emily that spring, we used our backyard. In spite of the medical equipment that had taken over the living room, there was still something inviting and warm about my house that made it the chosen location for a fifth-grade group of girls to do handstands and cartwheels, for the boys to shoot hoops in the driveway, and for music to stream from my pink boom box while we all ate cake. My mom lounged in a beach chair, next to her garden, glowing beneath the sun, hardly seeming sick at all.

Another day, in the middle of fifth grade, I heard girls at school talking about when they thought they would start their periods. At home, I had noticed the boxes of pink tubes smelling like fake flowers that were stacked in our bathroom cabinet, but I sensed I was missing key information I hadn't picked up from Judy Blume.

My mom spent the day at my grandma's house, a place I knew as well as my own. She lived less than a mile away from us, and we went back and forth between her home and ours several times a week. I loved going over there. It was larger and nicer than ours and filled with snacks. My mom was in the bathroom. I knocked on the door, bursting with questions.

My mom unlatched the door.

"Why are there periods, and when will I have one?" These words all but exploded from my face and were followed by tears. The shame I'd bottled up at school for not already knowing the answers to these questions had forced me into action.

She hunched on the toilet, and I realize now, through the wisdom earned by time and motherhood, my mom was having the kind of bowel movement people with colon cancer have, which is to say painful and bloody, and something she would have preferred to do alone. But there I was, almost eleven years old, tearful, curious, and trusting only one person to answer my questions.

I sat on the floor as she patiently shared information that made me lightheaded, her fingers twirling in my hair. As she spoke, I stared at the shiny brown tiles on the floor and the white grout lines around them, searching for a pattern that would never reveal itself.

OCTOBER 2011

Lemonade

Did you guys talk to Dad last night? Danny had sent a message to Brittany and me early in the morning. They'd texted back and forth a dozen times before I caught up after dropping Ben at day care.

I appreciated Danny's way of checking in first, indicating something was up, but not going so far as to break any news we didn't already have. My phone felt like a ticking bomb. Just fifteen hours earlier, everything had been normal. Now, the news about Lynch syndrome felt as urgent as a cancer diagnosis itself. I wondered which of us was carrying this mutation around. In my mind, at least one of us had to have it and at least one of us did not. These were magical thoughts, predicated on nothing but my dad's version of the letter Mary had sent, but I wanted a shortcut to the answers.

Reading my siblings' messages, wondering what to do next and what our relatives were doing with this information, I wished I had something wise to say in response, something that would make it all right or go away entirely. I was the oldest, but that morning, I felt even older than usual. Tired and separate and alone, even as my phone continued buzzing. I was the only one with a child whom I could have already passed it on to, making me feel like my stakes in all this were even higher than theirs. It wasn't a competition, but I felt certain there would be winners and losers, and guilty for possibly having continued this terrible chain.

Nothing about my life had changed in the past fifteen hours. I had Ben and Brian. My siblings and I all still lived within a mile of each other, with Brittany and me back in Lakewood near the house where we grew up. Danny was just on the other side of the highway in Cleveland. Our ages spanned only five years, but we were all in different stages of life. Danny was newly married, Brittany had recently moved in with her boyfriend, and Brian and I juggled our jobs and parenthood. When it mattered, though, we were all right there, physically and emotionally, and I loved that about us.

I was walking to my office, having what I imagined to be the only job in Cleveland perfectly suited for me as a project manager for a nonprofit organization that commissioned public art. I described it as the English major's way of doing urban planning, and most days I felt confident about my decision to be a working mother.

Usually, I loved arriving in Ohio City, where my office was located. I loved walking through the neighborhood, just across the river from downtown, visiting the food vendors inside the West Side Market. I felt comfortable on sidewalks bustling with people from all over the city, moving with purpose on and off buses, in and out of old brick buildings. But this day, I felt off-kilter, like the whole city was cut from paper and ready to blow away in an instant.

After graduating from college, I had secured an internship at Cleveland Public Art, a small nonprofit. It was only supposed to be for six months, but at the end of that time, my boss told me she liked me and offered to keep me on. I decided to apply to graduate school for urban planning and set my sights on Boston.

Brittany called me one day and said, "No offense, but if you want to do city planning, why would you go somewhere that doesn't need you? Don't you think it would make more sense to do it in Cleveland? Where you can actually make a difference?"

I felt like that was her way of telling me she didn't want me to leave. Plus, I liked my job and coworkers, I was in my early days with Brian, and I could complete my degree at Cleveland State for the cost of a single semester in Boston.

I kept my internship at Cleveland Public Art throughout graduate school. Two years later, I completed my master's degree in urban planning, applying what I learned in the classroom to my projects and what I learned from my projects to my coursework. After graduation, I built my case for a full-time job. My job gave me the chance to learn about the people and history of a community and find artists to create works reflecting the values of a place. I grew adept at navigating the permit process in city hall and making presentations to the City Planning Commission, walking its members through the story of each piece of art and why it added value to the community around it. I learned to read construction drawings and site plans and brainstormed ways to package these projects with our fundraising team.

One of the great conundrums of my life was how much I loved it, yet how I could trace everything that made it special back to losing my mom. I wondered if I'd feel as close to Danny and Brittany if we hadn't gone through that together, or if any of us would have moved back to Cleveland. If I wasn't so miserable as a teenager, I wouldn't have looked for beauty beneath unturned stones, wouldn't have discovered my love of writing and the arts. I may not have found urban planning if we hadn't driven through Rockefeller Park on Cleveland's east side for two years on our way to and from the hospital, becoming familiar with this shabby two-mile green space filled with statues and gardens celebrating the different cultures throughout Cleveland or the dilapidated mansions overlooking it. I wouldn't have pressed my cheek against the cool window of our Ford Bronco, wondering what happened to the neighborhoods along the park, to the people who used to live there, or about the people who stayed, which wouldn't have made my work with public artists as strong. If my dad hadn't later gotten remarried and moved us to LaGrange, a rural town on the cusp of suburban development forty-five minutes west, I wouldn't have had a stepsister who would later introduce me to Brian.

It seemed fitting to discover that the lemonade I'd been making for years was squeezed from poisoned lemons. I usually escaped into my work and felt rewarded by items checked off my to-do list. I'd gotten promoted a couple of times, clawing my way up the ladder and taking on larger, more complex projects. Project management meant the list changed daily, but it signified progress, and I was good at figuring out how to take the tiny glimmer of an idea and turn it into a real project.

Today, I was supposed to be making a presentation of potential artists for a project in the Cleveland Public Library's downtown reading garden. But instead of scanning portfolios and imagining the stories different artists might tell in the public space, I read and reread the texts from Danny and Brittany, trying to find something reassuring to say in response to their questions about what, exactly, we were supposed to do with this information, and what did "Lynch" mean anyway?

The most unsettling thing about my dad's call was that it made sense of something that hadn't ever made sense before. Why she'd gotten so sick. So young. It rewrote so much of the story I'd told myself about my life and my past, like a missing piece to a mystery I didn't know I'd been trying to solve. The demon that had taken over my mother was a mutant created by her very own body. The possibility that it lurked inside me and could strike at any time was almost paralyzing. The same part of my brain that could picture an unbuilt artwork in a park allowed me to see myself getting sick and what it would do to my family, turning the kernel of a possibility into the future avalanche it might create.

I turned back to my computer, trying to focus. The blank pages of my presentation glared at me until I gave up. Finally, I emailed the geneticist whose name was at the bottom of the letter from my Aunt Mary. It was a brief message noting receipt of the letter she'd sent regarding my uncle and a request for additional information, absent my usual pleasantries and exclamation points.

Dr. Marcia Arenberg responded within minutes, noting that my family's information could be useful for both her research and my own health. She recommended we meet to discuss genetic testing and noted that all expenses would be covered by a research grant. Her signature showed an address just five miles away from me.

It was happening too fast. My Uncle Jeff had died only six months earlier. My dad called just yesterday. Ben was so young. Brian and I were trying to have another baby. I was suddenly human data worthy of a stranger's time and money.

Instead of replying to her, I typed "Lynch syndrome" into my web browser. I had no frame of reference for what I was dealing with. I didn't know what it could mean to test positive for a mutation on one's MSH6 gene because I didn't even know what the MSH6 gene was or what a genetic variance entailed.

I would later learn that genetics research focuses on risks and probabilities, but that morning, all I could comprehend was that people with Lynch syndrome had an 80 percent chance of developing colon cancer and a significantly higher-than-average risk for cancers of the uterus, ovaries, kidneys, stomach, pancreas, skin, and brain. Humans are made of approximately twenty thousand sets of genes, each holding a code for every chemical process within our bodies. These sets are composed of two copies of each gene, one from each parent. Our bodies are so clever they have specific genes called "mismatch repair genes," whose job is to fix mistakes made by our cells as they run all the systems that keep us alive.

One of my uncle's mismatch repair genes was faulty, meaning that bad copies of his cells were replicated, over and over, causing his cancer. This genetic anomaly is passed down dominantly, as inherent as brown eyes. Carriers were advised to begin yearly colonoscopies ten years earlier than their parents' age at diagnosis, and women were encouraged to consider prophylactic hysterectomies. My last colonoscopy had been right before my wedding, five years earlier. My mom was twenty-eight when she became sick. I was already twenty-nine.

Sunlight streamed in through the huge storefront windows, highlighting the dust I hadn't noticed before, now impossible to ignore. I closed my web browser and tried to get back to work. I should have taken the day off. But it was flu season, and Ben was always being sent home from day care with one virus or another. Brian and I hoarded our time off, never knowing when we'd need to stay home with him. But also, I'd always turned to school and work in the wake of bad news, proving to myself over the years that as long as I kept achieving my goals—good grades, a great college, grad school, the job I wanted, a family, a home—I was okay. But my empty presentation reminded me I was falling short.

I had always known my mom had colon cancer, but this laundry list of other Lynch-related cancers my web search revealed made me dizzy. The recommendation for hysterectomy once childbearing was complete felt impossibly final. How would I ever explain all of this to Brian? Just yesterday, everything had been normal. Now, my screen grew blurry. We had Ben, but I ached for a second baby. I wanted him to have a sibling, someone who would love him as much as I loved Danny and Brittany, someone to play with, someone to vent to when his parents drove him crazy.

We had been trying to get pregnant for seven months. I knew it wasn't that long, in a big-picture way, but I worried because I became pregnant with Ben so quickly, and this was different. Now, I wondered how I would ever make a conscious choice to have a baby if I could pass this mutation on. Or if I wasn't getting pregnant because something was already wrong.

My fingers wrote back to Dr. Arenberg and asked when we should meet, carrying the load for the rest of me.

SUMMER 1993

Horses

I rode in the passenger seat of my Uncle Eddie's black sports car, my stomach churning from the winding, hilly roads of Charlottesville, Virginia. Eddie was my godfather and my dad's youngest sibling of seven in their sprawling Catholic family. I'm not sure whose idea it was, but that summer I was staying with my aunt and uncle for two weeks to help with their new baby. Even though I was nervous, I was excited to get away from home. None of my friends went to summer camps or traveled alone to visit relatives, so despite my circumstances, it felt like I was doing something a character in a book would do. Being out on the road, twisting through the hills with my uncle, took my mind off my mom being upset she couldn't attend Danny's baseball games or my softball games, my dad's constantly pinched lips, and me trying to figure out whether it would be a good day or a bad one in our house.

"You gotta check out this band," Eddie said. He pushed a plastic cassette into the tape player and handed me the case to Pearl Jam's *Ten*. I recognized some of their songs from the radio, but not the entire album. I'd been slowly moving away from Paula Abdul and Mariah Carey but hadn't yet found music to replace the sugary songs that no longer spoke to me. Outside the car, the winding Virginia hills unfolded around us. Eddie Vedder's voice made my stomach tighten in anticipation of something without a name.

My Uncle Eddie was married to my Aunt Andrea, a bubbly blonde barely bigger than I was. Three years earlier, my mom had made me a beautiful forest-green dress as their flower girl. Eddie was just sixteen years older than me, so young we didn't even call him "Uncle." He'd played quarterback on his college football team, only twenty minutes from our house. My dad took Danny and me to his games when we were younger, and we cheered our heads off for the Baldwin Wallace Yellow Jackets. The cheerleaders were the sunniest, most beautiful ladies I had ever seen, and they tossed foil-coated chocolates in the shape of footballs to me in the stands. I pretended to like chocolate because I loved being Eddie's niece, in the orbit of his college life.

As we zipped through the hills, drums and guitars filled the car. For once, I wasn't worrying about anything. I felt light and invincible. I lifted the handle of the car door to see if it would stay locked when we were driving so fast. The door swung wide open, and the roar of potential danger overtook the music. Eddie turned to me, the same flicker of anger I recognized from my dad's face rippling over him, the same anger I often felt simmering inside me. We turned around another bend and the weight of the car shifted, slamming the door shut again. I was so careful at home. I couldn't believe I'd done something so stupidly careless and risky. I pushed the lock back down immediately, pretending the previous moment hadn't happened. Eddie must have decided to do the same. He turned the volume up another few notches, and Eddie Vedder reminded us we were both still alive.

While my uncle went to work each day, my Aunt Andrea and I spent time with my baby cousin. Andrea was even younger than Eddie, just fourteen years older than I was. She drew thick blue eyeliner around her blue eyes and drove a new Jeep Cherokee that smelled like baby formula. We walked their golden retriever and the baby around the dusty roads of their brand-new housing development, and she introduced me to a neighbor who had a potbellied pig as a pet. I loved everything about my time down there, from dancing around the house singing to baby Taylor to our field trip to Monticello and the University of Virginia. One afternoon, Andrea let me raid her closet, did my hair and makeup, and staged "glamour shots," posing me like I was taking senior-class photos. I immersed myself in her baby-name books, dreaming up names for my own future children. Taylor, with her bright pink cheeks and tiny mohawk, was the first baby I ever loved.

For two weeks, I wasn't a girl with a sick mom. I was just a girl.

One day, Andrea took me horseback riding, something I'd never done before. She rode when she was younger and missed it. Another redheaded girl in tall boots, roughly my age, was getting her horse ready to ride, first laying a folded blanket on the horse's back, then setting her saddle on top. Her confidence around the majestic animal made me see myself as the clumsy city girl I imagined she saw, if she registered me at all. I studied the girl as she led her horse out of the barn before hoisting herself up onto its back. The woman in the barn helped Andrea and me put our feet into the stirrups and pull ourselves onto our horses' backs. I felt tall and nervous, but proud. I could have never done this at home. I'd asked to take riding lessons at some point, but when I saw how much they cost, I never brought it up again. I loved the slow, careful way the horse carried me, and it was fun to do something so out of character and new with my aunt. The bundle of nerves I'd gotten used to feeling went quiet.

After two weeks, my aunt and uncle drove the eight hours back to Lakewood. Andrea tucked the baby-name book into my suitcase, and I pretended not to see it. I braided and unbraided my hair a thousand times and talked about everything except my mom, who I was afraid to see. The healthy, vibrant, laughing mother of my childhood had vanished, and I tried to pretend I wasn't mad at her for it. Earlier that summer, my grandma had taken her to one of my brother's baseball games. She felt sick and we had to leave early. "I can't even watch my son! I can't even drive myself! I can't even use the goddamn toilet!" She pounded on the car seat. I felt guilty seeing her like that, completely powerless and unable to ease her suffering.

They pulled into my grandma's driveway, and I realized how much I missed this cozy white house and the people inside. My mom's family had always felt more like my real family than the Grahams, who had scattered like strangers to different states. When I walked in the door, my mom sat in the old brown recliner that had belonged to my grandpa until he'd died the year before. My grandma and my Aunt Jenny, my mom's younger sister, were sitting with her, keeping her company and waiting for me.

After two weeks away, it was shocking to see my mom's skeleton barely covered by skin and clothes. I felt ashamed for having gone away, for laughing and pretending to be the kind of person who rode horses, for leaving her behind.

There's a picture of us from when I came home. I'm sitting next to my mom, my hair in a messy ponytail, wearing overalls, freckled and fresh, practically bursting with life. A human piglet squished next to my mom, whose robe draped over her frail, gray body.

I kept that picture for years, tucked at the bottom of a drawer. Each time I looked at it, I was reminded of those awful feelings, of my commingled guilt and gratitude—guilt for leaving her that summer, gratitude for the escape. At some point, I threw it away. At first I felt bad for getting rid of it, knowing how few photos we had of that time. Yet this one did nothing but take me back to when things were unraveling.

Not all memories are meant to be kept.

NOVEMBER 2011

The Playground

The latch on Ben's stroller was stuck. Brian and I were in the parking lot at Lakewood Park after promising each other we'd stop talking about the mutation for a few hours. It had been just over one week since my dad had called.

"I hate this thing!" I shoved the stroller at Brian, unable to handle even simple tasks, apparently.

"Dude, chill. I got it." Brian opened the stroller with ease. I'd been yanking on the latch to close it, not open it, two years of muscle memory forgotten.

Lakewood Park overlooked Lake Erie, the edge of Ohio and the United States. This Great Lake stretched toward the horizon like an open future. It was this lake that had brought my Grandma and Grandpa Mitchell to Lakewood from Marine City, Michigan.

The park was chilly that morning, and the lake reflected the somber aluminum sky. The November wind had already blown the leaves from the oak trees, making them stick figures, waving their arms in the air above us in warning. In the lake, angry metallic waves bumped against each other, boulders bobbing and threatening to become a mountain range.

Ben skipped over to the swings, his glowing red shoes seeking balance on the wood chips crunching beneath his feet. Brian and I pushed him back and forth, back and forth. "I heard there's an eagle nesting somewhere nearby," Brian said, breaking my trance.

I tilted my chin to the sky, hoping to see the eagle while exerting the minimum amount of effort. Ben's foot knocked into my chest, and a sharp pain shot through my breast. I swallowed a shriek and narrowed my eyes at the monster laughing in the swinging bucket.

"Don't you want to try one of those?" I slowed the swing down and pointed to the merry-go-round, the slides, the wooden benches. "We brought you here to play, and Dad and I are the only ones doing anything."

Ben shook his head, clearly enjoying his toddler power. The bruise around his eye had faded from deep plum to a bluish green.

As I pushed Ben and the wind twisted against my eardrums, my thoughts drifted to my Grandpa Mitchell's mother, who died when he was six. The Grandma Fannie I had known as my great-grandmother was his stepmother, a woman who lived well into her eighties. My family knows little about my biological great-grandmother Myra, whose death in 1938 at the age of twenty-eight was attributed to taking too many diet pills.

"She was a simple woman," my grandma had told me years earlier. And that was it. A simple woman, married young, often home alone with her two children, trying to stay thin and pleasing to her husband, a sailor, who was gone for weeks at a time. Until now, Myra had been just a name to me, a forgotten echo, barely a person. But now, her short life felt like a premonition. I pictured a dark-haired woman standing on a porch, squinting into the setting sun, her hand shading her eyes as the wind sent her hair and skirt in different directions. Did we have the story right?

I wondered now about my great-grandmother's gastric distress. Diet pills sounded eerily close to another generation's version of *She did this to herself*, these mothers becoming their own unimaginable scapegoats.

Did Myra slip away, her body becoming a wisp of what it had once been as she left behind her children, the same as her granddaughter would, fifty-five years later?

The same as I now feared I would?

Without real information, the story writing itself into my consciousness was that Lynch syndrome was worse to the women in my family than the men. If I was a carrier, my fate would follow theirs. Was already following theirs.

It was tough to decide if I wanted genetic testing. I had a 50 percent chance of being told I was negative for the mutation, which would absolve my worries. But I also had a 50 percent chance of testing positive, which seemed like a death sentence.

Brian and I continued pushing Ben back and forth, silently rehashing the same conversations we'd been having all week, assessing the pros and cons of my having the testing done. The geneticist had sent a lot of information in preparation for our upcoming meeting, most of which I understood in an intellectual way, but all of which was clouded by the fact that this was my life we were talking about. One hundred percent of my family members with cancer had lived with extreme pain before dying. If I had the bad gene, how would I be any different? What I understood was that regardless of whether I was positive or negative, I was already whichever one I was. It was just a matter of whether I was strong enough to know.

The possibility of a hysterectomy also loomed large in my mind, tangling my hope for another child with the guilt of having such a desire. What if something happened to me and I left behind the very kind of broken family I'd come from, leaving more damage in my absence? Brian and I had been pulled together by the stubborn belief we could make a bulletproof family, one shielded from the fractures of our pasts, and the gene mutation felt like I wasn't holding up my end of our unspoken bargain.

When we met, we were drawn to each other's survival instincts. Brian's parents' divorce had been preceded by years of fighting and mistrust. His dad owned the tavern in LaGrange, a watering hole for bikers and people who seemed to court bad luck by coming in almost daily. After dropping out of the Catholic prep school his parents had scrimped to put him through, Brian went to my high school for a single year. The first year I moved to town, we shared a lunch period, but we never spoke. I remembered him as the guy with hair tucked behind his ears and huge jeans. I couldn't have known then that even though he broke his mom's heart by leaving his Catholic school and enrolling in the public school across the street from his dad's house, he still spent almost every night with his mom and brother.

Despite death and divorce, we had so much fun together. We were defined by our pasts but determined to grow beyond them. Brian seemed to enjoy rehashing the events of his life and understanding how they led him to where he was. I, on the other hand, preferred to live in the moment, to let my past stay where it belonged—far away.

But Brian was good at listening to me, at asking questions, and reading me. Being with him made me feel whole again. He made me feel safe and seen in ways I hadn't realized I needed. Over time, we underwent an inosculation: two separate trees binding together into the kind of strong family we wished we came from.

Now we were parents, but it often felt like we were auditioning for the roles. We worked so hard to be everything we had longed for as kids, constantly proving ourselves worthy of the task. How could I ever choose to have another baby if, despite our best efforts, they might still face the same trauma that shaped my own childhood?

Ben lifted his arms, ready now to try the slide. His cheeks were ruddy pink apples from the breeze. As I pulled him from the swing, his arm swiped my jacket, and there it was again: a pain in my breast. I flashed back three years earlier, when I pressed the palm of my hand into my breasts several times a day, seeking their reassuring soreness during my first trimester with Ben. He laughed as he tottered over to the slide, glowing beneath the fall sky. I inhaled, and the cool air felt good inside my lungs. *If this is real,* I said silently to the gray sky, to my mom and my uncle and the universe, *thank you.*

I made Brian stop at a drugstore for pregnancy tests on the way home, shaking with possibility as the cashier rang me up. Brian and I huddled together in our bathroom, watching as a second blue line manifested in the window of my pregnancy test, creating a radiant plus sign.

I held my hands to my face, unbelieving and desperate to believe. "I've been pregnant this whole time," I said to Brian and to myself and to the bathroom's blue walls. If this tiny, brand-new pregnancy stuck, I would be spared from making any choices on the matter. It was like every negative test over the past seven months had been waiting for this moment, to give me something to hope for, something beautiful when I needed it the most. Brian wrapped his arms around me. I never wanted him to let me go.

SUMMER 1993

Cathedral

At the end of that awful summer, our house felt consumed by illness. A queen-size bed was pushed beneath the front living room window, a hospital bed stood alongside the adjacent wall, and an old refrigerator filled with medicine hummed in the dining room. I sat in our coat closet, dragging my fingers over the rough plaster that disguised the cracks in the walls, pretending the jagged texture was a cactus and I was alone in the desert.

It was strange to feel so lonely in a house buzzing with activity. My mom's caretakers and my aunts and uncles and grandma constantly hovered around her. Everything seemed urgent. Did she have the right medicines? Would she recover from the operation to stent her kidneys? Was any of this treatment actually helping? I couldn't tell. I sought out dark, quiet spaces. I'd never been to a desert, but my imagination ran wild that summer, transporting me from the house that no longer felt like home and into mystical landscapes I'd only ever read about.

The house was heavy, like it was sinking under the weight of so much sadness and fear. Hidden drawers were built into the molding along our kitchen floors, holding forgotten remnants of lives that sparked my curiosity. I loved the matchbooks, combs, and old coupons I found in those drawers and often rummaged through them, searching for clues I might have overlooked, something to tell me how this story would end.

One evening, Danny and I were in the kitchen washing dishes in our usual dynamic of laughing, fighting, and getting water all over the floor. We still had fun together, even though it felt wrong. From the living room, our mom called for us. She stretched out in the hospital bed, her thin auburn hair pulled back by a heavy gold barrette.

"Why are you having Sean wash the dishes?" She spoke with a flat, deep voice that didn't belong to our real mom. "I don't want anyone else in this house, and it's not his job."

"What are you talking about? Danny and I have been in there the whole time." The clip was pulling on one or two of her hairs, and though I wanted to fix it for her, I kept my hands at my sides. "And who is Sean?"

"Sean across the street. You shouldn't be having him do our dishes, and I don't know him well enough to have him in the house."

Danny caught my sideways glance, both of us unsure whether this was a joke or if she was hallucinating.

The next moment, the anger left her face. She leaned her head back on the pillow and closed her eyes. Her mouth fell open. I worried that she had died. I looked at my brother. A sickening realization engulfed me. She was never going to get better.

We left the living room and finished the dishes in silence, careful to keep the water in the sink. After wiping the counters and folding the towel into a neat rectangle, I pulled my bike out of the garage and raced toward Saint James, the church where I was baptized and the only cathedral I knew of. It wasn't our regular church, but I needed the biggest, strongest beacon of God I could find. I flew past the corner stores, the shops with apartments over top, a baseball field, Dairy Queen, people walking their dogs and pushing strollers. I ignored the signs in the crosswalks and my burning thighs, pedaling furiously toward the stone bell tower and its sprawling granite staircase, the strength of God radiating from this monument to Catholicism.

I took the stairs two at a time and pulled on the imposing bronze doors. They were locked. I jumped from the ledge and shoved my way between two prickly green bushes and knelt next to the church. Mulch poked my legs. I didn't care. I prayed and I cried with such force, my breath caught in my ribs and choked me. I pounded the stone walls, begging for her to get better, for the cancer to go away, to have her back to normal, for her to please not die. But I knew, somehow, it wouldn't help. I came to God to save my mother too late, my religious beliefs dissolving into the dirt below me.

How could I believe in God when my family was living this nightmare? My mom, who had beautiful auburn hair she wore in perfect French braids, who had the sunniest smile and white crescent moons at the ends of her fingernails? Who appeared to be best friends with all her friends and playfully scolded our dog for running away by telling her to stop gallivanting around the neighborhood?

Sickness implied the possibility of healing. Every day, my grandma told my mom she was doing great. My dad combed her hair and kissed her gently on the forehead. The hospital performed various procedures. But despite all this treatment, she was only getting worse. Accepting her imminent death scared me as much as her illness itself. Who else knew?

Kneeling outside the church, I wondered if I would feel happy when she was no longer sick, if crossing the gulf between my old life and the new one looming in my future would bring relief. Then a darker thought took hold: *What kind of daughter could think her mom might be better off dead?*

Emptied out, I rode home. I walked my bike up the driveway and brushed the dirt off my legs before crawling into the hospital bed beside her, the plastic mattress exhaling beneath me as I settled in.

NOVEMBER 2011

Morning Sickness

Ben squatted beneath our bathroom sink, eighteen inches away from me, as I crouched in front of the toilet. Just like with my first pregnancy, this one flooded me with relentless nausea. The acid burned my throat less when it was mixed with something, so each morning, I ate a graham cracker and waited for it to come back up.

"Can you leave, please?" I didn't mean to sound annoyed, but the words came out in my bitchy voice, not my nice one.

"But I want to see what happens." His voice was so small. The bruise on his eyebrow had faded into a green shadow.

"When I throw up?"

My little sadist nodded and pushed his Hot Wheels car around in a rainbow shape in front of him.

I wanted to pick him up and carry him to the bed where Brian was still sleeping, or, I suspected, lying with his eyes shut, pretending he didn't hear what was going on. Instead, I rested my head on the toilet seat and closed my eyes. The thing about this pregnancy was that I wanted it so desperately and was so fearful of losing it that complaining in any way felt like I would jinx it. It seemed like some kind of divine intervention to be pregnant at all.

Just a few days before my dad's phone call, I'd gone to a yoga class, the first one in months, and as I lay on my back at the end of class in the darkened room, I felt hot, wet tears sliding down toward my temples. I'd been sad about something—was it that I was scared I couldn't get pregnant? Was it a premonition of what was coming?

An outsize amount of my gratitude for this pregnancy came from the relief of not having to wrestle with decisions about whether to continue trying for a second child or how far I could go with medical interventions, like IVF to screen for embryos without the mutation. But I still didn't enjoy being pregnant. What I loved was the promise on the other side: another baby, one I could love properly this time, now that I knew what I was doing.

And now, there I was, sweaty and shaking with nausea I barely kept at bay. I threw up first thing in the morning and as soon as I got to work. If I had to drive to a meeting, I would grow hot and dizzy and need to find a toilet before being able to talk normally. Knowing I was still pregnant offered a glimmer of relief, but it wasn't helping that day.

I wanted this pregnancy to be perfect. I wanted to drink green smoothies and eat lentils and transform my potentially mutant body into a perfect vessel of health. I clung to the idea of controlling my body, desperate to keep rogue cells from colonizing my colon. Dr. Arenberg insisted that while healthy, whole foods were best, my diet alone couldn't replace regular cancer screenings. I aspired to eliminate all animal products, but my body craved red meat and would settle, sometimes, for rotisserie chicken from the grocery store. It was the strangest thing, to be hunched over the toilet one minute and obsessing about a hot Italian sub afterward.

As much as I hated throwing up throughout the day, it also reassured me I was still pregnant, that I wasn't making the whole thing up. My ultrasound showed not only a strong heartbeat but a normal-looking uterus. It was reassuring to be pregnant. To be healthy enough to be pregnant. I'd heard stories of women discovering they had cancer when they were pregnant, but in spite of all the other doomsday scenarios playing out in my mind, that one stayed at bay.

Even still, my body refused to vomit with my son close by. "Baby, I need you to leave," I said to Ben. I couldn't imagine how my mom, with three of us, had gone back to school, become a nurse, and battled cancer. I was barely taking care of one child.

Ben looked up from his car, and tears pooled in the bottom of his hazel eyes. His chin puckered.

Suddenly, I realized how stressful the last couple of weeks had been for him. Brian and I had been having serious, tearful conversations that we tried—but clearly failed—to hide. How scary it must have been for him to see me bent over the toilet, making horrible noises as I threw up my graham cracker before beginning my day. What I had dismissed as morbid curiosity was actually his fear. I was back in the bathroom with my mom, needing her more than anything in the world and remembering how when she was happy, we were happy. Without noticing, I'd made our house stormy for weeks.

I reached across the tiles for his marker-stained hand. "Baby," I said, forcing myself to really see him, even though I wanted to close my eyes. "Mommy's not sick." I hoped with every inch of my body this was true. "There's a baby growing inside of me. It makes my tummy very sore."

Ben squinted at me. "Can I see it?"

I'd always been self-conscious about my stretch marks and squishiness, but I lifted my shirt and showed him my abdomen, which didn't look much different than it had a few weeks earlier. I placed his hand just below my belly button, to where it was harder than usual, as my mouth filled with saliva.

"I think I feel it," he said.

I kissed him and squeezed his sticky hand. "Please, please go snuggle with Daddy for a few minutes now, okay?"

Ben was barely out the door when my stomach retched. Chunky bile burned the back of my throat. I felt unfit in every way.

OCTOBER 1993

Love Letters

On a Friday in early October, my Aunt Jenny met us at our house after school. With tears in her blue-green eyes, she told Danny, Brittany, and me that our mom was having a particularly rough day. My aunt, whose contagious giggles had been quiet for weeks, suggested that we each write our mom a letter or draw her a picture and bring them with us to the hospital that evening. Jenny floated around the house, wiping our counters and folding the blankets on the empty bed while we wrote our letters. I wondered if, somewhere, our mom had tucked away letters telling us how proud she was of us. Jenny drove us to the hospital in her gray Ford Tempo. A coconut air freshener hung from her rearview mirror.

When we walked through the door to her room, I saw that our mom's bones were barely covered by skin anymore. Her hair was dead grass on the pillow. I read my letter, telling her how much I loved her. My words caught in my throat and I choked on my tears, but I made myself read the whole thing. I put my head on her chest, as hard as a wooden table. For as certain as I'd been that she was dying, there was nothing that made it any easier to see up close. Her heartbeat echoed inside my ear, and her breathing was shallow and quick, reminding me of my own breath when my dad wanted me to calm down. I hadn't known how to keep living with her like this, but I also didn't have any idea how to keep living without her at all. A tiny bit of wetness glistened outside her closed eyes.

My mom was still alive when we left, and I wondered if we'd see her again in the morning. Jenny was married to my Uncle Pat, whose three sisters picked us up from the hospital that night. They took us back to their house. My brother, sister, and I were puppies curled together in their guest room overnight, and when we woke, these sweet women had the horrible task of telling us our mom had died as we slept.

"Honey, I'm so sorry," they whispered in our ears with their soft arms wrapped tight around us. They drove us back to the hospital, where we met my dad, who stood next to us as we said goodbye to our mom.

Attempting to keep our lives as normal as possible, we all went to school on Monday. There was nothing normal about any of it, but I was relieved to be away from home. I tried to brush Brittany's knotty hair and slid into one of my mom's sweaters before curling my bangs with precision. That day, a well-intentioned junior high guidance counselor came into our classroom to deliver a lecture on loss. My cheeks smoldered as she shared, without my permission, my most private, devastating secret. It was the beginning of the school year, and most of these people weren't yet my friends, having come together from ten different elementary schools. Among the thirty kids who now knew I was a freak with a dead mom, only three knew my mom had been sick at all.

When the counselor asked if other students had experienced loss, one boy raised his hand and said his pet rabbit had died. I looked for a sign on his face that he was joking, but he was completely serious. I looked for other people to mention their grandparents, great-grandparents, anyone at all. I'd already lost two grandparents, three of my four great-grandparents, and I couldn't believe that in this entire classroom, not one other person raised a hand. My family was not normal, I was not normal. I was already an eleven-year-old who had sprouted boobs, who had bright orange hair, whose freckle-flecked face had been masked behind glasses for the past four years. I stood out too much already, and sitting through this nauseating lecture made me want to wither into invisibility beneath my desk.

A boy named Colin, whose mom had joined mine on most of our elementary school field trips, came up to me in the hallway later that day as I switched books out of my locker.

"I'm really sorry about your mom," he said.

I shrugged and told him, and myself, in my breeziest voice, "Thanks, but it's okay."

~

Later that week, we sat in church, the Lutheran one where my parents were married, where I had been a flower girl twice, and where we had held my grandpa's funeral exactly one year earlier. I had never seen it this full. The sanctuary was packed with faces I didn't recognize, all wearing the same expressions of shock and sadness. I didn't know my mom even knew this many people.

My eyes kept returning to the coffin. A white cloth was draped over it, with flowers resting on top. As the pastor spoke, trying to make sense of Julie Graham's death, I watched tears drench the faces of hundreds of people I'd never met before. I felt the unbearable weight of the most private loss imaginable, yet it was strange how our family seemed to be there to offer comfort to others, as if we were the ones holding everything together. I wondered where they'd all been the last couple of years, if any of them had delivered the meat loaves and tuna casseroles I hated. Why, out of all of them, was my mom's body enclosed within the casket? I crossed and uncrossed my ankles in the pew. I folded and unfolded the program, feeling like we were all on display.

After the service, there were snacks in the church basement. Later, our house filled with friends and relatives, all crying and talking to me in their fake-nice voices. I didn't want to see any of them. In fact, I didn't think I ever wanted to see any of them again for the rest of my life. One of my aunts on my dad's side told Brittany there was a baby in heaven who needed a mom, so my mom was now in heaven caring for the baby. I could tell she was trying to be kind, but a violent surge vibrated inside me, demanding I get my sister away from this horrible lie. I needed to be anywhere else in my house but near her. Brittany was six at this time, and I wove my bigger fingers into her smaller ones as we tiptoed up the creaky wooden stairs to her room. We played with her dolls, and my chest was a radiator, screeching to life as every chamber and pipe inside me filled with heat.

I stared at the wallpaper my mom and I had chosen for Brittany's room before she was born, its columns made of pink hearts, green dots, blue lines. The designs darted into each other, almost dancing. My aunt was dead wrong. I hated her and her explanation. If there was a God, it didn't decide to take my sister's mom away from her. From us. How dare she suggest we were the kids worth leaving behind. Because some dead baby needed her more than we did? Why wasn't she in heaven with the ghost baby instead?

~

We buried my mom several weeks after the church service at Rosehill Cemetery in East China, Michigan, in a plot next to the one my grandma would someday share with my grandpa. After the burial, my grandma's family spent the weekend on Fawn Island, a quiet retreat filled with weekend homes located on the Canadian side of the Saint Clair River, directly across from Marine City, Michigan, where my grandparents had grown up.

A man piloting a powerboat ferried travelers from Michigan, and ten minutes later, we arrived at Canadian customs, a paper-filled one-room office. After customs, the boat moved slowly through an internal canal system, dropping us off at the dock in front of the cottage. There were no stores or shops on the island, so everything needed for the weekend had to come with us on the boat. The cottage's front walls were dominated by two-story windows, ensuring constant river views. A coffee table in the living room held books identifying the ships that moved cargo down the Saint Clair River and the native birds. It impressed me that my grandma knew the name of every single ship that passed by, having watched them for most of her life.

Time slowed down on Fawn Island, with the first couple of hours spent unloading groceries, making beds, setting up croquet in the backyard, and shedding the feeling that you were supposed to be doing other things. The cottage was far enough away from Cleveland that we didn't go very often, and when we did, it needed to be for at least a long weekend to make the trip worthwhile.

My Uncle Jeff made sure the spindles on the fishing rods moved smoothly and brought Styrofoam containers filled with dirt and worms. Brittany stood on the wooden dock in bare feet, her bright yellow hair whipping around her face in the wind, throwing out her line into the canal. She caught dozens of sunfish, expertly removing the hooks from their lips while Jeff held them with a towel and rethreading her own hook with fresh worms. She amazed me, this sister who wasn't afraid of anything.

There was a park on the island along the Saint Clair River where we spent an afternoon playing catch with a football. The game quickly escalated to seeing who could punt the ball the farthest. The river's swift current and icy waters always made me nervous. My grandma had swum across this mile-wide expanse as a teen, her feat a constant metaphor for her strength and stamina. I was more accustomed to the lazy rivers trickling into Lake Erie that almost dried up in the summer, not this powerful channel carrying cargo ships throughout the Great Lakes.

During the game, the wind caught one of Danny's kicks, carrying the ball out into the river. On an ordinary day, this would have ended the game, our ball floating down the river like a duck. But today, my dad seemed determined to prove how alive he still was. Without hesitation, he stripped down to his briefs despite the biting cold and dove into the nearly freezing river, swimming after the football as it made its way to freedom. For a few moments, I wondered if he'd just decided to swim away, and then felt guilty for even imagining it. A couple of minutes later, we cheered as my dad emerged from the river, victorious.

My mom would have turned thirty-one that weekend. Her absence created a calm that moved in like fog, a peaceful daze I was afraid to blink away. I wanted to stay on Fawn Island forever, transported from the uncertainties of my real life and into a musty cocoon of time-stopping quiet. I listened to John Lennon sing "Watching the Wheels" over and over on my Walkman, his gentle voice filling up my empty spaces. Through my dazed stupor with the water rippling all around me, I didn't care if I ever saw my friends, my house, my school again. He was trying to persuade himself to let things go. But like me, he wasn't ready. I didn't want to let her go.

I was ashamed for picturing my life without her, for even thinking it would be easier at all. One day, toward the end, she had asked me to make her a bagel. She preferred cinnamon raisin bagels, toasted, with both butter and cream cheese. I was mad at her that day, for everything from how bad being sick made her smell to how helpless and lost I felt in the midst of it. I was angry, I was eleven, and I was lazy. I toasted her bagel, but I only put cream cheese on it, assuming she wouldn't notice. When I brought it out to her, she took one bite before throwing it at me, so angry that I didn't even love her enough to make her a bagel the way she liked.

My legs dangled over the dock outside the cottage, and I wished I had made that stupid bagel the way she wanted it. As I sat there, my dad came out and plopped down next to me, our legs hanging over the canal. He put his arm around me and we cried, watching the water shimmer under the moonlight, or through our tears.

DECEMBER 2011

Family Tree

Dr. Arenberg was based out of the same hospital that had treated my mom and Uncle Jeff, which was also the same hospital where they both died. The day of my first appointment, I drove from my office across town and through Rockefeller Park, the same green space we'd passed through to visit my mom when she was sick. The hospital was in University Circle, a neighborhood packed with museums, colleges, and health-care institutions. Nearby, a public art installation made of stones traced the path of a former Indigenous trade route, marking the spot where a buried stream flowed underground. It was strange how one place could hold such a patchwork of memories.

I parked on Euclid Avenue and walked past the taller, newer hospital buildings and toward the older, pale yellow one bearing the address from Dr. Arenberg's email. It wasn't until I approached the entrance that I realized it was not only the same hospital system but the exact building where we'd visited my mom and my grandpa in the preceding years. It seemed quaint, nestled into a side street, like it had been designed to fit into London a hundred years earlier and now sat like an overdressed relic amid a row of parking garages and boxy medical offices.

I was nearly eight weeks pregnant, aware every day of how much I wished for everything to keep progressing as normal. Like with Ben,

I was nauseated all the time. Unlike with Ben, I found it strangely comforting. As long as I kept throwing up throughout the day, I could believe the baby was still alive inside me.

As I walked toward the yellow building, a different feeling of sickness than my constant nausea spread through my limbs. I was young again, walking into this hospital with my dad. I'd asked him if my mom was dying exactly once. He'd answered, "She could outlive any of us," which I think he thought would give me hope for a miracle but instead made me afraid that I might come home from ice-skating with my friends to find our house in flames or accidentally jump into moving traffic. Though I'd lived with awareness of my mortality for nearly two decades, walking through the door of the hospital to learn the potential limits of my life felt like reaching a point of no return—a destination with no path back home.

But the email had been very clear: This appointment was not to conduct a genetic test. It was just to discuss the testing process. Brian had offered to come with me, but I told him to save his time off. The deeper truth was that I needed to face this on my own. I needed space to understand and process and figure out how to handle the information in a way I could manage. I knew I couldn't shield him from it forever, but I wasn't ready to share the burden. First, I had to make sense of it myself before I could take on the weight of his reaction too. At the same time, I imagined an alternate storyline where this entire thing was a big misunderstanding.

I made it through the maze of hallways and to the correct waiting room. A tall man wearing a sweater-vest introduced himself as Lou, the genetic counselor who worked with Dr. Arenberg. "She's the best," he said as we walked to a small gray room with a table and four chairs. The bright white winter sky was framed by windows at the top of the walls. Boxes of tissues sat on every available surface: table, windowsill, counter. I didn't think I'd be able to work with people who cried every day.

Dr. Arenberg entered the room a few minutes later. Her wildly curly hair was somewhere between black and gray and balanced by her glasses and smart-looking slacks. Her prominent nose and jaw reminded me of my Grandpa Mitchell. Lou took a seat beside her and folded his hands on the table. One of them had only two fingers, suggesting the origin of his interest in genetics, but I tried not to let my eyes linger on them.

"Your uncle seemed like a wonderful man," Dr. Arenberg said, sounding friendlier than I had expected. "I'm sorry I didn't meet him under different circumstances."

"Me too," I said, forcing a polite smile. Jeff took up a lot of space in every room he was in. This wasn't only because he was physically imposing, which he was, but because he was also among the funniest people I knew in real life. He would have found a way to make me laugh in here, in spite of everything. I understood why there were tissues everywhere.

"I'm looking for families that have HNPCC, or Lynch syndrome, but don't meet the current standards for testing." She slid a blue sheet of paper across the table with a matrix of different cancers, ages, and percentages. At the top it read, "Hereditary Nonpolyposis Colon Cancer (HNPCC)." I felt healthy, but maybe I didn't even know what healthy felt like. I wished I was in the wrong place, or the wrong person, that this entire chain of events was a mistake.

Dr. Arenberg continued. "There's something called the Amsterdam Criteria, which are the current guidelines doctors use to recommend testing among families with hereditary cancers." She spoke slowly and sought eye contact with me. "I'm not convinced the current guidelines are catching everyone who may be impacted. Does this make sense?"

I nodded and looked at Lou, whose presence I still wasn't understanding. I felt him studying me and wondered what he saw.

"According to the Amsterdam Criteria," Dr. Arenberg continued, "there needs to be three relatives who have been diagnosed with colorectal cancer. For you, Jeffrey was only the second relative. Your mom being the first. I'm so sorry for your losses, by the way." She made a note on her pad. "But your grandfather had what we call a Lynch-associated cancer. So my research team is looking for families who would fall under a broader set of guidelines for testing. We want to educate doctors about these revised guidelines. Which brings me to you."

"I know this is a lot to take in," Lou said. He and Dr. Arenberg reminded me of listening to a couple tell a story they've shared dozens of times, each one having their part. His calm demeanor was at odds with his large frame, as though he'd spent his entire lifetime trying to appear smaller than he was. My heart echoed inside my eardrums, close to the same rhythm as the second hand ticking itself around the clock on the wall behind them. I'd later learn that Lou was an expert at using space at the end of his sentences as a way of encouraging me to talk, but in this initial consultation, I was waiting for him to continue. I needed all the information available to me before committing my thoughts to words, especially when the stakes felt so high. I didn't feel like a rational person weighing my options. I was angry and frazzled, like I wanted to stomp my feet and shout, *This isn't fair!* But at the same time, I wanted to prove to them I had my life together, that I was exactly the kind of person they sought to help: an upstanding member of society, a good mother, someone who deserved to keep living.

"I'm here to help you navigate this process and make decisions along the way that are best for you," Lou said. His role as a genetic counselor wasn't to study genetics itself, but to provide therapy to patients who were considering genetic testing. He seemed to be offering emotional support to balance out the cold, hard science that Dr. Arenberg doled out.

"We'll start by drawing your family tree," Dr. Arenberg said. A folder with Jeff's name on it sat beside her. Lou pulled out the chart and placed it next to the blank paper in front of Dr. Arenberg.

"We can't just use his?" I asked, looking toward Jeff's papers.

She shook her head. "I like to have one for everyone. Never know what we might learn." She started by writing Jeff's name and drawing a box around it.

He was my mom's younger brother, the third of four Mitchell children.

Jeff became sick two years ago, when Ben was a baby. During his chemo, Ben and I spent the day with him. Ben was a year and a half old that autumn, and we hadn't seen Jeff as much as I would have liked during his short life. I was a new mom, cramming five days' worth of work into the four days each week I was getting paid. Brian was in night school, getting his master's in education, with Ben's birth being the catalyst for his desire to gain more control and options in his teaching career. We were in the thick of early career struggles and new parenthood, collapsing at the end of each day, golden rays of hope in our chests that this stage was building toward a more fulfilling future.

It was a Monday, my day home with Ben. I wanted to see Jeff, but I was nervous. His cancer scared me. He wore a port under his shirt, chemo dripping into him while he moved through the rest of his life. I'd heard through the family rumor mill that his chemo leaked one night, creating an apocalyptic scene of my Aunt Mary dealing with the spill. I envisioned her in an astronaut-style suit, cleaning a nuclear site.

Jeff and I ended up spending the entire day together. We laughed and talked, time moving faster than I wanted it to. I made us sandwiches for lunch, and Ben played with Jeff's multiple remote controls. My grandma told me later that it took Jeff nearly a week to figure out how to get his television back up and running properly, but it had been worth it for the good time.

Right after the New Year, my Aunt Mary mailed out invitations for a party celebrating Jeff's victory over cancer. The invitation featured a picture of him from a day of fishing on their boat, his bright green eyes glowing.

"Does this feel like bad luck to you?" Brian held the invitation out in front of him, as though the paper itself had cancer.

On a Saturday the following April, Danny and I visited Jeff at the hospital together. He was supposed to be moved up to the intensive care unit that day but was never stable enough for transfer. Like at the party a few months earlier, many people showed up to see him that day—maybe, like us, sensing the end was near. I felt guilty that I hadn't seen him since his party, but as we milled around the waiting room, I learned he had intentionally withdrawn from his family and friends, choosing to spend this time on his own. His room was directly adjacent to the waiting area. Visitors came expecting, I assume, that we would check in quickly and head back out. Yet few, if any of us, left. The waiting room filled with friends, coworkers, and members of his church, all of us passengers waiting to board an airplane to an unknown country. There was a gravitational pull on all of us, an unspoken sense that we were waiting to learn something more final.

Brian kept calling, asking me when I'd be coming home. "Soon," I'd said each time. Each time lying. Ben was supposed to stay overnight with my mother-in-law, and we had plans for a rare date night. But I couldn't bring myself to say out loud what seemed to be happening, choosing through my silence to have Brian be annoyed that we weren't getting ready to go out rather than face the truth of why I wasn't home yet.

Unable to pretend to him any longer, I said, "I can't leave." I cried softly into the phone. "Can you come?"

As we sat in hospital purgatory, my Aunt Mary spent most of that day in the room with Jeff. Periodically, she came out to ask a specific person or people to come sit with them. Danny, Brittany, and I were called together, and I was surprised by two things. The first was how lucid he was. He was unable to talk, but he nodded along with us as we chatted with him, his eyes soaking us in. The second was how massively distended his chest appeared. His chest cavity was rapidly filling with fluid as his tumors grew and put pressure on his lungs.

Around ten o'clock that night, Mary stood in front of us and said, simply, "Jeffrey is rejecting intubation." Her voice cracked as she brought her head down toward her knees. He had days, at most. More likely, hours. Mary's sister and family were there to hold her hands and stroke her hair. I'd never felt the absence of cousins so sharply—my mom was the only one with children.

Jeff's side huddled around my grandma, whose head bowed over her lap. "My heart," she said, "is broken." Even as I watched her curl into herself with grief, I knew I'd never be able to forget the sound of pain in her voice. It felt, in that moment, like she was losing again every single person she'd ever loved. I remembered how unbreakable she'd seemed to me as a child, and I understood for the first time how good women were at putting on strong faces. As I put my hand on my grandma's shoulder, I was strangely relieved she didn't feel the need to hide her pain, that she trusted us, as adults now, to help support her.

Back in the gray room with Dr. Arenberg and Lou, I circled Jeff's name and age on the paper in front of me. It was suddenly clear why my grandma had lost two of her children to the same disease, both far too young. Like realizing the culprit in a mystery, I felt silly for not seeing the clues earlier. Dr. Arenberg drew lines from Jeff's name to my grandparents and his three siblings. It was surreal, watching a stranger create a map of my relatives. She knew where the ravines and valleys were and was showing me terrain I should have known better.

She reached across the small table and placed her hand on mine.

"Even if your mom had swum daily in a pond of carcinogens, without a genetic mutation, she wouldn't have gotten cancer so young." She waited for me to look at her before drawing the lines from my grandpa's name to my mom's. "We are recommending you get genetic testing. If you choose not to test, we suggest you follow the screening protocols for people who test positive."

"It can be hard, however, for many people to get these tests covered by insurance without having proof of the mutation," Lou said.

"So, I would need to get colonoscopies every year and consider a hysterectomy and all of that, with or without the testing?" I asked. Suddenly, not getting tested no longer seemed like a valid option at all. Pandora's box had been opened, and there was nothing I could do to stuff this information back inside.

"Yes, that's what we would recommend," Dr. Arenberg said. "There are, of course, people we meet who choose not to move forward with us. But the average age for the onset of colorectal cancer with people who have Lynch syndrome is between forty-two and sixty-one. I think your uncle has given you a great gift," she said.

Even among a population of individuals at increased risk, my mom was an outlier. My long-held belief that I had survived a lightning strike was suddenly replaced by an overwhelming feeling that I lived in an electrical field. My family was lightning itself.

I grabbed a tissue and wiped the mascara-streaked tears from my cheeks, ashamed of worrying about how I looked in this room built for sharing bad news. It was strange, having the events of my past suddenly click into place, making more sense than they ever had before. At the same time, I didn't want any of it to be true. I was torn between wanting to return to the time when I believed I had already survived the worst and my new understanding that this was a place that had only seemed safe. I felt a certainty inside my core that I carried the same mutation, that the innocent polyps I'd had removed over the years were the ominous markers of something far bigger.

Dr. Arenberg turned the sheet toward me, silently asking me to fill in my dad's name next to my mom's. I wrote "Dan." My parents had always been "Dan and Julie." Their names melted together like a song in my mind. From my parents' names, Dr. Arenberg drew a line to Danny's. My younger brother, my constant playmate. He'd struggled with Crohn's disease since his early twenties, a different affliction of the colon. I asked if it was connected to Lynch syndrome somehow. She shook her head. "Bad luck," she said.

She drew a line to Brittany's name, my wise younger sister, always carrying a camera and finding beauty in the most ordinary things. After our mom's death, we'd all found our own ways of surviving, discovering what and who we loved. It seemed like the mere act of turning over these stones was unsettling something, bringing old fears and bad omens into the light. We were all doing so well. I didn't know why I had to sit at this table and mess it all up.

Dr. Arenberg wrote my name and drew a line to Ben's. My son was almost three years old. He loved construction equipment and superheroes and sports. My body was heavy in the chair. I gripped the cool metal bar on the sides. The letters in his name swam on the white paper.

I was no longer the child who had lost her mother. I became the mother who would be lost, leaving a hole inside my son he would never be able to fill. I couldn't imagine causing him that kind of pain, and right then, I knew I would do whatever Dr. Arenberg told me I needed to do.

Sixteen years after losing my mom, I became one. When I was in labor, my mother-in-law, Suzie, wiped my face with a cool rag and kept Brian grounded so he could hold one of my legs each time I pushed. Brittany was there too, offering sips of ice water between contractions. Before going into labor, I had imagined only Brian and the doctor present when our son was born. But after sixteen hours of labor, when it came time to push, I begged Suzie and Brittany to stay. I never registered how much my mom loved me, or how much my grandmother loved her, until I pulled my slimy newborn onto my chest. Waves of love and fear washed over me, unlocking a universe I hadn't known existed. In that moment, I understood these women in a way I never had before, as though time's long arms were welcoming me across an invisible threshold.

In caring for newborn Ben, I learned that love isn't just an emotion but a verb, a series of actions repeated day after day. His needs were as constant as the tides. At first, love felt like a primal instinct, a ferocious drive to keep him safe, connecting me more to the animal world than to the moms I met at the breastfeeding clinic I visited. Over time, though, emotions unfolded within my heart for this beautiful, perfect, helpless creature Brian and I had created. We called him "the Brad Pitt of Babies," amazed we'd made something so wonderful.

Mothering Ben also connected me across time with my mom. I imagined her learning to love me, a puny pink blob with orange fuzz on my head. I pictured her pacing the rooms in our duplex or passing me off to my dad for a nap. Somewhere within the maze of diapers, feeding, learning to use a breast pump, getting an IUD placed, and sunrise walks with a stroller and our dog, I finally felt how much she must have loved me. Until I had Ben, I hadn't understood how hard it must have been for her to stop being the kind of mother she wanted to be.

Facing the reality of this mutation was another practical act of maternal love. Before I sat down to work on this dreaded family tree, I saw my mom's death in terms of what *we* lost: me, Danny, Brittany, our dad, our grandma, her siblings, her friends. But as I traced the lines connecting her to me, and me to Ben and the unborn baby inside me, I began to understand the depths of what *she* had lost. I felt the fear, sadness, and guilt that must have consumed her as she contemplated all she would soon leave behind. Sitting in this orderly room with two strangers, I felt an unknowable anger beginning to unclench its invisible claws. For the first time, I understood how far beyond her control it all had been.

THE MID-NINETIES

My So-Called Life

The summer after my mom died, my dad drove us all down to North Carolina for a weeklong visit with his best friend. We slept in his driveway in a borrowed conversion van, its back seat folding out into a makeshift bed. During that week, I pieced together fragments of my dad's conversations and realized he was testing out this city like a new pair of jeans, seeing how it fit. I overheard him plotting his next steps over backyard beers—contemplating packing up his kids, the only pieces of his life worth keeping, and starting over somewhere fresh. I buzzed at the possibility of leaving everything behind, imagining I could transform myself into a completely different person. At the same time, I couldn't imagine making new friends. How would I ever be able to explain my life to them?

We didn't move to North Carolina. We went back to Lakewood, but I also felt myself craving and fearing change as a restlessness consumed me. I wanted to talk about everything my family had experienced, but I didn't know where to begin, or whom to share it with, or what words to say. I continued getting good grades, and my grandma still came over before and after school. I kept the same friends and played the same sports and went to the same catechism classes. No other volcanoes in my landscape erupted. Everything was the same, except it all seemed hollow and pointless. I felt this inner force bubbling inside me, giving me a parallel existence next to my real one.

As empty and awful as not having a mom anymore was, it also made me feel special. Despite my misery, I was chosen for this particular life and, therefore, I could bear it.

When I thought about my friend Emily, whose mom once threw a plastic bowl at her for behavior that wouldn't have been a punishable offense in my house, or Sarah, an only child in a house that was so quiet, or Amanda, whose mom had also lost her mom when she was young, or Lindsay, whose dad berated her mom in front of me when I stayed for dinner, it was impossible to explain what disorder in the universe made me the one who had lost her mother. But so keen was my need for a silver lining, I made this loss into a superpower. I never voiced this belief, but the notion that I was operating on a different level carried me through the chaos of my grief. I knew what truly mattered and what was petty, and this sense of clarity gave me the strength to grasp that middle school wouldn't last forever. Nothing did.

In eighth grade, we were assigned a semester-long group project, and the smartest boy in our class was placed in mine. The task was to transport top-secret government property from Cape Canaveral to Phoenix. Each group had to pick a project manager, and I assumed mine would choose the genius. To my surprise, however, they elected me. I assigned everyone their roles and turned in my journal each week describing the process. I understood that if I wanted two class clowns to do what I asked them, I just needed to get one of the popular kids on my side. When one of my best friends wasn't pulling her weight, I assigned another friend to keep tabs on her. I loved managing this project and figuring out how to motivate everyone else. I was inexplicably good at planning for the unexpected problems we might encounter. As part of my disaster planning, I budgeted for our team to haul an emergency vehicle in case our trucks broke down.

When my team was announced the winner, one of the judges said it was because ours was the only team that included alternative transportation. At the end of the course, my teacher noted how wonderful it was to watch me blossom as a leader. I knew she was being honest because I felt it myself. Focusing my nervous energy on this project revealed talents I never knew I had.

On Thursday nights, I practiced basketball with a team of girls who went to Catholic school. Afterward, I stood outside with the winter air on my hot legs. I didn't mind the cold. I did mind that I was always the last one waiting in the parking lot to be picked up and that I wasn't tall enough or fast enough to be anything more on this team than someone who played a few odd minutes while the best players caught their breath. But it felt so good to run. To make myself sweaty. To have a point of focus. I loved studying our plays and trying to guess where the other players would go, understanding the game happening inside of every game, which always seemed to be a matter of who wanted something more.

After showering, I made popcorn and watched *My So-Called Life* with my dad. Sometimes the show prompted awkward conversations about what his high school years were like. I wasn't sure if he actually enjoyed my TV show or if he just wanted to spend time with me—or maybe it was both. With him there in the dark living room, I kept my thoughts on a short leash. I didn't let my mind linger on Jared Leto's hotness, or my curiosity about the different characters' comfort levels with drugs and sex, or the intersections between the nerdier kids from stable homes and the cooler ones with broken families.

One day, while vacuuming the couch cushions, he found a list of my goals, one of which was to "have a perfect body." My dad told me I was beautiful and that the only woman in the world with a perfect body was Jamie Lee Curtis. I pretended not to remember writing this list, but his words stuck. It gagged me to think about him noticing women's bodies at all.

My own sadness was one thing. My dad's grief was another, and I didn't want to see it. One morning as he poured low-fat milk into his coffee, he told us that instead of drinking the liquor he stored in the china cabinet, he had poured the bottles down the utility sink. I scraped peanut butter across my toast, feeling I was supposed to be proud of him, but I didn't want to know these things about him. I could tell he was trying to make me open up—but I'd gotten so good at keeping my thoughts to myself, at saving my insights for my schoolwork or friends, that I never knew what to say.

I didn't want him to know things about me either. How in the aftermath of losing my mom, I wondered obsessively about things that felt forbidden, like when and with whom I'd have my first kiss. It felt almost sacrilegious to entertain such thoughts amid the overwhelming grief. But I couldn't help it. I weighed myself a dozen times a day, scrutinizing the unfamiliar reflection in the mirror, aware of a body I didn't recognize, one that seemed to crave touch in ways I couldn't yet understand. Those feelings, in the sad quiet of our motherless house, filled me with shame.

~

My dad met Margot through our mom's friend Kathleen, at a party she was hosting. In the shadow world between childhood and adulthood, I gleaned that my dad's relationship with Margot severed his friendship with Kathleen and her husband. When I was fourteen, they got married and built a new house on a new continent forty-five minutes away in a town called LaGrange. Margot came with a sixteen-year-old daughter, Kim, and two cats.

At the same time, I was learning my own lessons about love and heartbreak. I had my first boyfriend that year—a genuinely sweet boy who was so smart he went to Lakewood High School for his math classes. We shared first kisses, but when school ended and we were no longer walking home together, we had little opportunity to see each other. Then there was another boy, one who played guitar and had long hair, who kissed me with such softness and urgency that I thought of little else. We talked on the phone for hours, until I was practically asleep with it in my hand. I explored the fringes of my virginity that summer, feeling both excited and disgusted by myself.

When I found out he had started seeing someone new, I didn't go home for three days. I called my dad from my friend Kayla's house each night, promising I'd be home the next morning. But I couldn't bring myself to face him—or the bedroom I'd soon be packing up. Kayla's parents were divorced, and her mom hired someone to watch her younger sister during the summer days, giving Kayla, and all of us who rode our bikes to her house, endless freedoms.

I nursed my broken heart while Kayla smoked cigarettes. I cried while we watched *The Real World*, *Clueless*, and *My So-Called Life* reruns on MTV, each one over and over. Kayla's room was dark, and she had a cat who nibbled my hair while I slept. Eventually, my eyes dried out, and as I stepped back out into daylight, I realized—with clarity so crisp I nearly went back inside—I had not been holed up with a broken heart because of some boy. I didn't want to move away. Everything I knew was in Lakewood. My grandma still lived just a mile away, we saw my aunts and uncles all the time. I knew every crack, corner, and crevice of our house. Our mom's stenciled borders were still at the tops of our walls, there were still corners of the closet that smelled like the rose-scented powder she liked. She may have been gone, but her essence was everywhere. Moving away meant leaving her too.

Danny didn't want to go either. "You guys don't even love each other!" Danny screamed at our dad. "I don't care if you get remarried, but in my heart, I know she isn't the right one." I was proud of my brother for, as usual, voicing what I felt but was afraid to say.

I tried poking holes in my dad's plans using reason and educational metrics. "I'm in honors classes, and they only have one honors course in the entire school! Did you even consider the school district when you looked at real estate out there?" What I couldn't say was that even though I didn't want my dad to be miserable anymore, I didn't believe my future stepmother would make any of us happier. She seemed to be the exact opposite of my mom. Where my mom was warm and fun, Margot was cold. Small, blond, and fitness obsessed, she proudly displayed actual glamour shots of herself in her suburban condominium.

We made brownies together once, and I mismeasured one of the ingredients. Instead of shrugging and figuring out a way to troubleshoot, she said, "Now I just know I can't trust you with these things." It seemed like such a needlessly cruel reaction to an honest mistake, showing me it was she who couldn't be trusted.

In the end, our dad did what parents have been doing throughout time—making the decision himself, leaving us with no choice but to go along with it. After a small ceremony at city hall in July, the day after Brittany's ninth birthday, Danny, Brittany, and I stayed the weekend with our Uncle Jeff and Aunt Mary. It seemed like the end of an era. Margot had taken me shopping for a dress, being sure to note that most of the summer colors washed me out, and I couldn't believe this was really happening. My Uncle Jeff grilled steaks, and Mary made twice-baked potatoes, which might have been the most delicious thing I'd ever eaten to that point. We stayed up too late watching *So I Married an Axe Murderer* and laughed way too hard. They drowned us with love and attention that weekend, and I soaked in every drop of it.

They took us out on their boat, soaring across Lake Erie while we were towed behind on an inflatable inner tube. There was a safe zone for the tube, a V-shaped space between the wakes created by the boat. If you stayed within this space, it felt like you were gliding, a seagull cruising above the water. By shifting your weight to one side, you could ride up onto the wake. Usually, we wiped out attempting to crest the wake. But, sometimes, with our weight balanced just right, we'd crest the wave, flying across the open water, holding on for dear life.

~

The new house had five bedrooms and a two-story living room that the construction drawings called a "Great Room," and sat on a dead end overlooking a soybean field. The developer assured my dad the field would become a golf course soon. At first, my dad and Margot seemed to genuinely want to blend our two families. During the early months in the new house, though, the facade began to crack. My dad claimed allergies to her cats, who were first banished to the basement before being given away, causing my stepsister, Kim, great distress. This led to our dog being sent to the basement until she walked outside two days before our first Christmas in LaGrange and died, right there in the driveway.

The love we had grown up with was so constant, it was invisible. But in the new house, I felt its painful absence. This big house provided space for all of us to retreat, together yet distant, bound only by an address. It felt expansive yet hollow, without the nooks and memories we once had. This place, without history or connection, seemed to magnify the life I'd left behind on Rosewood Avenue. Sometimes I wondered if the ghosts of our former selves were still rambling through, looking for the pieces of ourselves that stole away.

~

My new stepsister, Kim, had an electric-blue Chevy, and although I secretly thought the car was tacky and something I wouldn't be caught dead driving myself, it was our ticket away from the sterile new house. One day after school, we drove past the older houses near the small downtown, past miles of cornfields and cow pastures, until we reached a mobile home park. Driving past the Welcome to Pheasant Run sign filled me with more fear than any of the neighborhoods I'd encountered in Cleveland. The yards outside the mobile homes teemed with people drinking and smoking in the middle of the day. It was the kind of place I'd only seen in movies and never expected to be myself.

"It must be that one," Kim said, peering out the window at a group of guys wearing baggy jeans and shirts emblazoned with metal band logos. They looked like grown men, and I was suddenly self-conscious about my plaid pants and polo shirt, acutely aware of how tightly it pulled across my chest.

"Come on, they're all here," she said.

Kim had fully embraced her fresh start at a new school, seizing the opportunity to build the types of friendships I'd left behind. She'd cut her long blond hair to her chin and dyed the front of it blue. She covered her walls with posters of Kurt Cobain and adopted a tarantula named Sabbath, which she fed baby mice. She acted tough, but I remembered her as the shy girl she was when our parents first got together and appreciated the commitment she made to her transformation. She was also my only friend so far in LaGrange and was proving much better at fitting in than I was. Kim pulled down the visor, checked her hair, and pouted in approval.

My stomach fluttered like it did before visiting the dentist. I put on my Dr Pepper–flavored lip gloss and dragged myself from the car, forcing a smile.

We walked past a wall of guys holding cans of beer and cigarettes, up the stairs, and stepped inside a room filled with smoke and screaming music. A couple of guys had girls sitting on their laps, grinding themselves into their grimy jeans.

"Is Zach here?" Kim asked a guy wearing quilted pants and a visor.

"Oh, hey, Kim, cool. What's up?" The guy pointed down a dark, narrow hall.

"Come on." Her fingertips reached for mine, guiding me behind her.

A group of kids I recognized but had never spoken to sat in a row on a mattress with crumpled sheets and a semicircle of metal folding chairs facing the bed. They passed a bong between themselves, the first one I'd ever seen in real life. Zach lifted his eyes and waved Kim over to him, sliding her onto his lap. He opened his mouth and pulled her face into his, exhaling the smoke between her teeth. She nuzzled into him like one of her cats, and I felt more alone than I'd ever been. I knelt on the dirty brown carpet and crossed my hands over my lap.

Someone passed the bong to me, which I couldn't pretend to know how to use. I shook my head. He said, "Here, I'll hold it for you. Just breathe in from this hole as much as you can." I didn't actually want to get high, but I also didn't want to draw attention to myself, so I stuck my face into the chamber and it filled with smoke. As soon as I breathed it in, I was choking. I coughed so hard I feared I'd throw up or crack my tooth against the glass.

"Oh, man, that means you got a great hit," the guy said. "I miss being able to cough it in, again and again." He put his hand low on my back. I froze completely under this stranger's touch in this foreign room and quickly stood up. The entire room spun around me as I walked out. I steadied myself by holding my arms out and touching the hallway walls.

The bathroom had a murky window that let in just enough light so that I didn't need to find a switch. I leaned into the sink and stared at the figure in the mirror. It struck me, as I hid in there, that I had lost my mom in stages. First, we lost her as a mother as her mind slowly faded. Next, we lost her body. After we moved, we lost the constant closeness with the rest of her family and the comfort of living inside the walls she had decorated. I splashed water on my face and looked for my mom in my reflection. I couldn't see her. This house, out here surrounded by nothing, was an earthquake about to swallow me whole, and I wondered how I would survive.

"Ethan thinks you're cute," Kim told me on the way home. I pretended I was too high to hear her as I stared out the window, across the cornfields.

DECEMBER 31, 2011

Long December

I zipped up a black dress—not technically a maternity dress, but one I had hidden in the back of my closet because it always made me look pregnant. It was my thirtieth birthday, and we were going to a New Year's Eve party. Brian and I usually hosted New Year's Eve. It started as a tradition with my best friend, whose birthday was December 21, ten days before mine. When we were in college and home for winter break, we started hosting dual birthday/New Year's parties, and I loved the excuse to make my birthday festive under the cover of a bigger holiday.

I was just on the cusp between my first and second trimesters. I'd finally stopped throwing up, but my uterus had kicked into high gear for this pregnancy, and I looked much further along than I actually was. The last thing I felt like doing was cleaning up after a bunch of happy drunk people, so I was grateful to have somewhere else to go.

Thirty was an invisible milestone, one I hadn't realized I'd put on a pedestal until I arrived at it. When I was eleven, I thought thirty was old—or at least old enough. I still remembered the surprise thirtieth birthday my mom had thrown for my dad. He pretended to be mad about it, but I could tell he was secretly happy to be worthy of a celebration. As the middle of seven kids, he always seemed overshadowed to me, swallowed up by the sheer number of people in his family. He didn't even have a middle name, as if my grandparents couldn't be bothered to come up with something to go along with Daniel.

Now, as I entered my thirties, my mom seemed so young. I couldn't remember how we had celebrated her last birthday. That absence sat like a stone in my chest, but there was nothing to be done about it. And so I got dressed up, did my hair and makeup, and promised to be the designated driver for a group of our friends. My best friend's sister was hosting, and it felt good to get out and be regular people for the night.

Party food has always been my favorite food, so I enjoyed the freedom of eating whatever I wanted that night. I filled little plates with olives and cheese, and it felt normal and fun to be out, talking to people about unimportant things and laughing. I hadn't realized how long it had been since I'd laughed.

Just before midnight, our host passed out glasses of champagne, and I held one in the air with everyone else, counting down the seconds to the end of a year that had asked so many questions but offered no answers. When the room erupted with shouts of "Happy New Year," Brian kissed me. I took a single sip of champagne and continued cradling the glass between my fingers.

"Hey!" A man's unfamiliar voice rose above the rest of the party sounds. I turned my head to see who was talking. A broad-shouldered man with short dark hair was making his way toward me. He pointed a finger right in my face and then at my stomach. "You," he said, "shouldn't be allowed to have babies."

"What?" I looked at Brian.

"What the hell is wrong with you?" Brian asked him.

"Someone should call CPS," the guy said, his words slurring together.

A woman with a bright pink face came up from behind and put her arm around him. "I'm so sorry," she said, more to Brian than to me. The woman placed her small hand on her husband's back and steered him away in the manner of wives. He shook his head at her, embarrassed, and I was forgotten.

"Do you know that guy?" Brian asked, visibly shaken.

"I've never seen him before in my life." The moment was over, but adrenaline coursed through my limbs. His anger pierced me. One of the things that embarrassed me about being pregnant was that people felt entitled to make comments about my body. It was impossible to be inconspicuous. But it was more than that. Even though there was something sad and desperate about the guy, he was also like some sort of drunk prophet reading my soul. Maybe I shouldn't be having more kids, with or without this potential mutation. Maybe there was something fundamentally wrong with me that made me a bad mother, something my own mother might have recognized if she were still alive, something I'd never be able to pick up through books or osmosis or determination alone.

"I should have punched him," Brian said. Something flashed across his eyes like he'd welcome a fight. "You good?"

I swallowed the lump growing in the back of my throat and mimicked the other wife, placing my hand on his back. "I'm fine. Just let it go." I wanted to leave, but also to be calm and cool, the rational good mother. I'd spent the past two months lost in my own troubles, trying to protect Brian from whatever might be down the road. I knew I'd get testing, but it felt like there was so much practical groundwork to cover first—namely, surviving the holidays and then getting life insurance I might no longer qualify for. We were stuck in a holding pattern, with the threat of bad news looming like a storm cloud on the horizon. It hit me then: I wasn't protecting Brian from anything. If anything, he wasn't faring much better than I was. I'd just become too withdrawn to see him.

Brian went back to our friends, and I wandered into the dining room for more chocolate-covered strawberries. My friend who was hosting came up to the table next to me.

"I have to apologize for Mike," she said. "He's usually the nicest guy." She took a sip of wine and leaned in closer to me. "Do you see his wife, Heather, over there?"

I followed her gaze into the next room, where the pink-faced woman stood among a cluster of other people I didn't know. Heather looked as regular as anyone I'd ever seen. Brown hair, pale winter skin, a well-fitting dress, at least a few years older than I was. "She's had three miscarriages this year." My friend spun a metal charm at the bottom of her glass. "They've really been through it."

I looked closer at Heather. I saw someone who exercised and ate well, someone who took care of herself. I turned away, wanting more than anything to give this woman the privacy of her own experience. I imagined the few friends with whom I'd shared my family history talking about me among themselves, their pity more than I could stand. I wondered where the other couple was in their journey right then. If, like us, they were deep in the unnerving uncertainty of it all.

I felt a connection to this stranger. I imagined her losing trust in her body and having no idea what was coming next, knowing there was no promise of a happy ending. But I had to give it to her, to both of us: There was nothing in our appearances indicating what we'd been through. No symbols pinned to the fronts of our dresses. Just two women living inside our skin, behind smiles that concealed the disasters and broken dreams lurking beneath.

I hoped this new year would be better for both of us.

THE LATE NINETIES

Am I Okay?

My favorite part of LaGrange was that we lived just eight miles away from Oberlin College. As soon as I got my driver's license, I took my homework to the coffee shop there, browsed the bookstore, and tried to see if I fit in with the students. I couldn't believe that one of the most well-known liberal arts colleges in the country was here in the middle of Lorain County.

While visiting the bookstore one day, I saw a flyer for a creative writing workshop for high school students at Kenyon College, two hours south of us. On a whim, I sent an application, and to my surprise, I was accepted. I'd been saving money from my job at a grocery store and spent two weeks in the dorms at Kenyon with other students from several different states. I hadn't even known I had so much to write about, but once I was in the workshops, words, ideas, and emotions spilled out of me. I'd never been around other teenagers who wrote. It felt, for the first time I could remember, that I was surrounded by people who were like me.

When we weren't in workshops, we wandered around the beautiful Gothic campus. There were sandstone academic buildings, colorfully painted Victorian houses, and acres upon acres of open space. I fell in love with the campus, but even more with the feelings it ignited inside me. Suddenly, I could envision myself as a college student. I could see a future that was completely different from the life I'd lived so far. I wanted to be surrounded by books and possibilities, around people who felt the same way.

I paid attention to the other participants in my classes. They all seemed to come from wealthy families, with parents who were trying to boost their college applications with extracurriculars designed to secure acceptance to schools like this and who could afford the cost.

I brought my dad and Margot down to visit when it was time to fill out college applications. I could see they thought it was beautiful—and also completely beyond our means. My dad tried to talk me into one of Ohio's state universities, but there was nothing he could say or do to change my mind. I applied, was accepted, and even qualified for financial aid.

While Kenyon was my goal, once enrolled, I worried I wouldn't be able to hold my own academically. Despite getting through the entire college application process on my own, it seemed like I was at Kenyon by the skin of my teeth. Yet I *did* hold my own, soaking in every drop of knowledge coming at me from seminar-style courses, and I was grateful each day for the education I received.

Among the things that amazed me about Kenyon was that the dining hall and student health-care clinic were free. If I had been a young homeless person, it would have been the ideal place to pretend I belonged. With tuition so high, these necessities were baked into the college experience. Birth control was just five dollars per month, available without hassle from the health center. Condoms were everywhere—every bathroom stocked with candy dishes full of them. That students would sleep together was a given. The real imperative was making sure we didn't destroy our futures in the process.

One day while I was waiting for my birth control prescription to be filled, I noticed a flyer about counseling services. The college offered free support for issues like anxiety, eating disorders, and trouble adjusting to college life. I didn't set up an appointment that day, but the seed of an idea took root.

Aside from one awkward session with the hospital social worker before my mom's death, in which I was asked to draw my feelings, I had never talked with a professional about her. I spent the last seven years proving that I was okay—better than okay, even. I'd gotten into Kenyon, and I'd handled blow-out fights with my dad about student loans and the value of a liberal arts degree. I applied to both an introduction to poetry workshop and for a position as a student associate for *The Kenyon Review*, the college's acclaimed literary journal. I was accepted by both, earning some external validation.

But.

Did I want to talk to somebody? Was counseling an option for me? Was I who I was supposed to be? The Grahams were do-it-yourselfers, making and fixing our own problems. A few days after seeing the flyer, I was in a friend's dorm as she sorted through her color-coded closet. I knew she was in counseling and asked her about it. She said her counselor was amazing and I should totally see her—whether I thought I needed therapy or not.

~

As it turned out, there were a lot of students who wanted to talk with counselors. I added my name to a waiting list. By the time I finally had an appointment, it seemed a little silly to go. I was doing fine. Better than fine. My grades were strong, I loved my classes, I'd found a group of friends who seemed more like friends and less like people sitting in the same room together.

I went anyway. Ruth was quiet, had silver hair down to her chin that she tucked behind her ears. She wore long skirts and long necklaces and long sweaters, layers upon layers of cozy calmness surrounding her. She also had a dog with black curly hair that followed her around campus and put its head in my lap when I sat down in her office. Instinctively,

I reached to scratch behind its fluffy ears, my fingers jarring loose how much I missed having a dog. I was crying before we even started.

"I'm so sorry. I love being here. I don't even know why I'm crying. It's just . . . my mom died, a while ago. Am I okay?"

Over the course of several sessions, Ruth asked me open-ended questions about myself and my life, and I worked to decipher my actions and my intent over the last several years. I had been so focused on getting out of LaGrange, and I felt guilty about leaving my sister and brother. Being a high achiever had been such a distraction that even when I was home, I had an excuse to disengage. Brittany, apparently, had cysts removed from her head, and I only knew about this later. Had I not been told, or did I not care enough to pay attention? I needed validation: Was I a good person? Was I a normal person?

Nobody in my family, not even my grandma, ever asked how I was doing. My well-being was assumed and accepted without question. I felt like the kitchen I grew up in, built for keeping secrets. Little drawers everywhere, designed to tuck away the ugly scraps and memories we didn't want but needed to store. I barely even knew my mom. How could I miss her so much? How could I take all the pieces of my life and make them into something, into someone, worthy of love and goodness?

The gifts Ruth gave me were the space and courage to talk about myself. For all my self-absorption, I was perpetually afraid that if I looked too closely, I'd discover that losing my mom had broken me—that I was just a shell, collecting good grades and striving to be "good enough" without truly knowing how to love or be loved. I wondered if I was still myself, whoever she was. Ruth helped me see I didn't have to be anyone different. She also confirmed there were countless ways I could have responded to my mom's death, and the way I did was just one of many that were normal. She told me I was okay and, somehow, I began to believe her a little more every day.

WINTER 2012

The Dam

After meeting with Dr. Arenberg, I took home the blue paper with all of its statistics and set it next to our toilet, where Brian and I both saw it multiple times a day. For weeks, I obsessed about my odds of having the mutation, fixated on a question no one seemed able to answer—or perhaps I wasn't asking it in a way they understood. How would the statistics change if I tested positive and followed their treatment protocols? *If* I had the mutation *and* I did annual colonoscopies, were my odds of getting colon cancer still 80 percent? Or did they drop to 0, 20, or some other number?

The best answer they gave me was, "We don't know yet."

When I shared this information with my dad, he said, "Remember, all doctors are careful to say they *practice* medicine. They don't make promises with medicine or offer guarantees of any kind." He wasn't totally on board with me getting tested. He wasn't opposed to it either, but he also wore his skepticism like a suit of armor. I felt his worry through the phone, for me and my siblings' health in general, and for me being pregnant at this precise moment in particular.

Facing his worries on top of mine was more than I could carry. My own fears already consumed me, infiltrating every part of my life, like the codes encrypted in DNA. It seemed like every story I'd told myself had stopped being true. I was no longer someone who had survived something. I was now someone who had to face things larger than I could handle. I was still Ben's mom, still Brian's wife. I still went to work every day. But I was also young again—scared and grieving my mom's death in a way that seemed fresh.

Each morning, after dropping Ben off, I cried alone in the car. I dreaded the prospect of no longer being able to drive him and couldn't remember the last time my mom had driven us. I thought of how her independence had been stripped from her, how she had needed help all day with everything. It seemed awful and unkind that I hadn't understood this before. If only I'd known more about life, I could have helped her so much better. That winter, I felt like I lost her all over again—but this time as an adult daughter, not a child. I missed her and mourned the relationship we could have had. As I contemplated my own future, I finally found compassion for her. Feelings I hadn't allowed myself to feel for years surfaced like invasive plants, greedy for sunlight and oxygen, choking out the parts of me I'd worked so hard to cultivate.

Every week, I went back to the gray room in the yellow building to see Lou, the genetic counselor who also served as a therapist. Lou became the bucket I poured my anxiety into so I could function as a human mother, worker, and wife outside his office. He explained that genetic counselors do not recommend testing for diseases unless the information could improve the prognosis. "We wouldn't test you for something we couldn't somehow treat," he said. I wanted him to boil this all down into something black and white, but he would only offer nuance.

Though my pregnancy made me exhausted to my core, sleep eluded me during the weeks I waited for my testing to be done. My arms would fall asleep at night, and I'd jolt awake from dreams of seeing my mom again after years apart. Each time, I'd have to tell her she was still dead. That my dad had remarried, we'd moved away. There was nothing left for her to return to. But then, she would die again anyway, and that was when I'd shoot awake, arms tingling, and creep downstairs, a living ghost haunting my own life.

I couldn't sleep. I couldn't have drinks with my friends or with Brian. I couldn't keep moving, the way I always did: stripping decades of paint from our oak front door, renting a tile cutter to lay down a new ceramic floor in our foyer, scrubbing the tops of our cabinets free of cooking grime. My pregnancy forced me into a stillness. I had no choice but to lie with the grief I'd pretended not to have, like it was a letter I'd stuffed into a bottle, sent to sea, and found waiting for me at a distant shore. I lost my mom again and again in these months. In fact, I think I lost everything I'd ever lost again, decades of unfelt feelings pressing against a dam that finally collapsed.

Every day, I came home from work and lay on the couch or in the bathtub. I didn't want to play with Ben, or cook for Ben, or read to Ben. The simplest things took such great effort. One day, when I was in the bathtub, a race car came in underneath the door. It was followed by a dozen more, one after the other. There was a knock.

"Mom?" Ben's tiny voice called through the door.

"Yes?"

"Somehow, a bunch of my cars are in the bathroom." He opened the door, holding an empty plastic bin.

He placed each car in its slot and pulled out the red stool he used at the sink. He sat next to the door. "I'm just going to make sure nobody bothers you in here."

There he was, my sweet, perfect boy, the one I would do anything for, once again making sure I was okay. This seemed wrong in every way. I wasn't even sick, and yet I was withdrawing from my own life. I was barely taking care of the child I had. What business did I have with another one?

I asked Ben to cover his eyes and peeled myself from the bathtub. Wrapped in my towel, I found Brian. "I think I'm scaring Ben," I said, squeezing my head between my palms. I wanted to be a normal pregnant person, imagining the baby's nursery, or the engaged mom I used to be, fingerpainting and playing hide-and-seek. I wanted to feel like myself again.

"You will, you will," Brian said. He looked worried too, though, like he was trying to convince himself as much as me.

I met with Lou so that I could be brave and positive with Brian. But here I was, sitting in the gray counseling room, no longer keeping it together at home either.

By the time I sat in Lou's office, Brian and I had built millions of memories together, each one now feeling precarious. I imagined everything good in my life dissolving or erupting, my entire childhood replaying itself with new characters.

I ached for my mom, not the idealized version I'd known as a child or the woman other people had described to me, but the multifaceted person I was only now beginning to understand. Before I knew Lynch syndrome existed, I pictured myself as someone who overcame obstacles and had emerged gracefully, my scars invisible to the world. Now, the possibility of being the sledgehammer that demolished my family made me wish I didn't exist at all. I felt certain my mom didn't want me to remember her by her worst days but by her best. How would I be remembered if I got sick?

I felt like a fraud who didn't deserve any of the good things I had. When Brian and I fought, he was usually the better person, willing to say he was sorry first. As soon as I felt the iciness thawing, I could apologize too. But how could I ever apologize for my potentially broken genes? For my inability to handle any of it? There was also the baby, whose nervous system I was certain I was frying with my own worries.

Sitting inside Lou's office, he reminded me that even if I had the mutation, it wasn't something I had done.

I nodded and blew my nose. I felt myself moving in circles, rehashing days and years, wondering whether I'd ever feel normal again. I knew I needed to have the testing done, but I was unable to take any steps forward until I faced the grief I had buried for so long.

AUGUST 2003

The Northeast Blackout

My dad stood in the great room, dwarfed by its cavernous ceiling and the tall windows that loomed over him, his arms crossed tightly over his chest. I planted myself by the kitchen table, hands on my hips.

"I spent my entire life working to get out of those neighborhoods!" he shouted. Beyond the edge of our backyard, the soybean field rippled in the wind.

"I hate driving back and forth every day!" I yelled back. "*You* chose to move to the middle of nowhere!"

"It's not safe," he said. "I can't have my daughter living there."

Back and forth we went, each of us certain in our positions. It was a routine we knew well, each of us challenging the other. He, solid in his belief that he knew better than I did. Me, positive he was holding me back from becoming who I was meant to be. I'd been back in LaGrange for eight months, finished with college and desperate for what I imagined was my real life to begin. I'd started seeing a guy I really liked and was beginning grad school in downtown Cleveland in a few weeks. Earlier that day, I'd signed a lease for an apartment in an old Victorian home near my internship. I hadn't sought my dad's opinion on the matter but was informing him now.

"I can't study urban planning and live out here! I'd be such a hypocrite!"

"I don't know why you're going to school for that anyway!"

Our fights were never about a single thing. Whether they were about where I'd go to college, what I'd study, who I dated, or why I never told him anything about my life, they all seemed to boil down to a battle between my drive to find out not only who I was but who I might become, and my dad's drive to provide me with the life he wished he'd had. I was the same age he'd been when I was born. I couldn't see how hard he'd worked to raise me, how much he gave up in his youth, how he'd been parenting for exactly half his life and for practically his entire adulthood, how terrified he must have been to let me go. I didn't have words yet to explain how badly I needed space to figure out my future for myself.

He grew up in Cleveland, at East Eighty-Third and Union, in a neighborhood filled with immigrant families living in small houses crammed together. They went to school at the Catholic church several blocks away. His parents, six siblings, and his grandma shared a four-bedroom house with a single bathroom. I can see, only now, how he craved space to move and sky around him.

Back and forth we went, me criticizing his decision to move to LaGrange and him criticizing my desire to live in a city and wasting my potential on a master's degree without financial security.

"You'll be back!" he shouted.

"I'm *never* moving back here!" I vowed.

No sooner was this promise out of my mouth than the clock on our stove buzzed and went black. The fan spinning above my dad slowed down. A minute later, the power burst back on, the stove and microwave both beeping as they came back to life.

The air between my dad and me was so thick with self-righteousness, I was certain our screaming match had caused the power surge. After briefly blinking on, the lights dulled for a few seconds before giving up completely. It became quiet.

When we opened the front door, the rhythmic hum of crickets and cicadas engulfed us. There were no lights inside any windows. Neighbors came out onto their stoops, looking up and down the street for signs of power they wouldn't get back for several days.

The argument was paused. I went back into the house and grabbed my purse, vibrating with the need to leave.

"I'm meeting Chrissy and Amanda tonight," I said. I was also meeting the guy I liked, Brian, but he was still so new and fresh, I kept him to myself.

My dad grabbed his flashlight, the same heavy club-like one he'd bought me for Christmas. He wanted me to keep it in my car to use if I needed to change a flat tire or to bash someone over the head. It wasn't dark yet, but he was preparing, as always, just in case.

"Be careful," he said. I knew he meant *Be careful driving*, but there was something about the way he said it that seemed to be about everything. Be careful on the highway, in my new apartment, in the city, in a life he'd never pick for himself.

FEBRUARY 2012

Drawing Blood

By February, we were deep into Cleveland winter. Everything outside was cold, gray, slushy. Dr. Arenberg and Lou warned that I might not qualify for life insurance if I tested positive for Lynch syndrome, so a man from a life insurance company came out to our house with a clipboard and a traveling kit of medical supplies to take our vitals, weigh us, and talk about family histories. Brian and I were both approved for thirty-year policies, which seemed so far off at the time.

I still visited Lou every week. My belly continued growing, as though my uterus contained a living talisman I carried with me everywhere. The acuteness of Lynch syndrome had worn down to a dull, consistent pulse.

One of the coping mechanisms I developed sometime in college was to choose a future date and tell myself, "By then, I'll have already made the presentation / installed the project / completed that report / et cetera." The frustrating or difficult task will have already been finished, and I trusted I'd do what's necessary to reach that point. Now, I started thinking, *By spring, I'll know.*

I scheduled my blood draw for March, right before Ben's third birthday. The date was circled in a red leather book filled with work meetings, doctors' appointments, and playdates. Instead of being in my usual old, yellow building, the blood test took place in one of the wings of the hospital itself. Walking among real patients transformed me from a healthy person assessing my options into a sick person seeking treatment.

I found where I was supposed to be, and a nurse walked me back to a room where the walls were decorated with pastel animals, storybook characters, and the alphabet. I was four-and-a-half months pregnant, and being in this room for children nearly took my breath away. I imagined parents holding their babies on the paper-covered exam table, cooing at them to be still, promising it would hurt only for a moment, praying for the blood to both answer their questions and validate their worst fears. I felt both their agony and the hope they laid at the feet of doctors. The babies and children treated in this room were sobering reminders that my situation remained hypothetical, that I was in the realm of statistical probability and not frantically searching for a diagnosis to either my own health problem or, worse, one of my children's.

This room squeezed me like a dress refusing to zip. Though my heart pounded and my eyes stung, I held out my arm, closed my eyes, and turned away from the nurse, afraid of my blood and the codes it held swirling inside the glass vials.

SPRING 2005

The Equinox

A couple years into our relationship, Brian and I took a walk through a nature preserve on a dewy spring Saturday and ended up veering toward the animal shelter. Sometimes on these walks we'd stop for a few minutes to play with the kittens we weren't allowed to have in our apartments. But on this day, we found ourselves captivated by a gray, fluffy puppy that a mailman had found on his route. The volunteers said he was an Australian shepherd mix, and he flopped around on the floor while we rubbed his belly.

We both wanted to bring him home with us, but neither of us were allowed to have pets. As we often did in those days, we tried to figure out a way to bend the rules, rationalizing how they didn't technically apply to our situation. "He could live with my mom for a few months," Brian said, "and when my lease is up, I can get a bigger place."

By the time the shelter reopened on Monday, we called to see if the puppy was available, but of course, the happy little guy had already been adopted shortly after our visit.

That night, we lay on top of the covers of the green futon in Brian's studio apartment, aglow from the light in his fifty-gallon aquarium. We'd known each other for two years by now. Kim, my stepsister, had run into him and gotten it stuck in her head that we'd get along. I'd had no interest in anyone connected to LaGrange, but I'd been back home after college and was just bored enough to reach out. He'd recently returned from a cross-country road trip and was just bored enough to call me back. We met for beers at a bar in Oberlin on a Thursday night in May, after the first public meeting I'd ever worked, both of us confessing we almost didn't show up. He had dark brown hair, but a light in the bar glowed blue above him, tricking me for a moment that his hair was dyed. The skin around his dark eyes crinkled when he smiled, which he did while he talked. I never remembered feeling so at ease with someone new.

When the bar closed, Brian and I walked around Tappan Square, the big town green space, until late night became early morning. Once we started hanging out together, we never stopped. After our tumultuous childhoods, our freshly hatched adult lives melded together as we clawed our ways toward the futures we envisioned.

Lying on the futon, I was quiet, afraid to put the growing ache in my stomach into words. At the same time, our honesty with each other was our compass. I was learning, as I continue today, how to let myself be seen under truth's bright lights. I started crying before I could speak.

"What is it? What's wrong?" Brian asked.

"It's just that . . ." I had to take a breath, pausing to be certain. "I want a life where that dog could've come home with us. I want the place that comes after this." There I was, scanning the horizon, swimming toward an impossible finish line. I wanted to hold on to the emotional safety he gave me—the space to be who I was, to talk for hours, to laugh together at life's absurdities, and for him to let me cry when I didn't know what else to do.

"Are you just now realizing this?" He rolled to face me. "I feel like I've been here for a while."

A few months later, right before the Fourth of July, Brian asked me to marry him next to Lake Erie. He knelt beside our favorite tree, a tall cottonwood that somehow grew where the break wall, waves, and sand came together. The crescent moon was so bright the tree cast a shadow on the shore. He gave me his grandmother's engagement ring. I loved knowing he'd had to ask his mom about this ring, that she must have believed I was good enough to receive it.

Fourteen months later, I stood at the back of the same church where my mom and dad got married, where we had the funeral services for my mom and grandfather. My dad stood next to me in a tuxedo. I didn't love the concept of "giving away the bride," but I also knew this tradition meant something to him. I'd joked with my siblings that the best thing to have ever happened to my relationship with my dad was my moving out. I wanted him to know how much I loved him, and I couldn't imagine not letting him do something that would make him so proud. Brian stood at the end of the aisle, which I'd never realized was so long.

"You don't have to do this if you don't want to," my dad said.

He wasn't questioning the marriage. At least, that's not how I took it. He was giving me one final out, just in case.

"I'm sure," I said, feeling the weight of the moment. I wanted to remember everything, but I could barely focus on any of it.

"I love you." My dad squeezed my hand. A few weeks earlier, he'd confessed that he and my stepmom would be divorced by the end of the year. She sat up front, in the pew my dad would share in a few moments. Brian and I had suspected something was going on with them. Every time we'd seen them over the past year, they'd alternated between civil frostiness and outright rudeness.

After my dad shared that they were splitting up, asking me to keep it quiet for the time being, Brian said, "I think we reminded him of what it was like to be happy."

I'd resented her involvement throughout our wedding planning, and now I hated that a woman my dad no longer loved sat where I wished my mom was sitting. Yet without her, my stepsister wouldn't have connected me to Brian. I was so aware of the strange lines of dominoes that fall throughout the world, each setting off unknown future events. But my dad was here. Brian's parents were here. My mom's favorite poem about the kindness of a smile was printed on the back of our programs. I wore opal earrings, her birthstone. I felt her with me and my dad, all the way until the high school quartet played the first notes of the song that meant it was time for us to start walking.

Brian and I made our wedding vows on the autumnal equinox, not for spiritual reasons but because it was the date our reception venue was available. Discovering we were getting married on a day when Earth is in perfect balance in its orbit around the sun felt like a gift from the universe. My sadness about going through this ritual without my mom was balanced by the profound joy I felt for making promises to keep loving Brian in front of our families and friends, for turning September into a month of happiness and not just a prelude to October's lingering sorrow. I was reminded on this day, as I had been for years before and would be for years into the future, that every joy is amplified by sitting right next to the sorrow that preceded it.

FEBRUARY 2012

The Waiting

My blood was shipped to Utah for DNA sequencing. During the three weeks it would take for my results to come back, we transformed our office into a nursery. Brian wore his painting clothes while the Grateful Dead echoed off the bedroom walls. I washed the hardwood floors and the white baseboards and sifted through the baby gear and clothes stored in the attic. It was hard to believe Ben was ever small enough to wear the outfits I'd packed away. We chose a sunny shade of lime green for the walls and grew excited about Ben having a baby brother. We dusted off the baby names we contemplated for Ben and tried them on this new boy, but none were the right fit. This baby wasn't simply the baby who wasn't Ben. He was his own being, and he needed his own batch of names.

On a Saturday afternoon, Brian painted "Thing 2" on the walls in the bright green paint, harkening back to when he had painted "Thing's Room" on Ben's light blue walls three years earlier. We laughed at the dripping letters on the wall and wondered who the heck our children would someday become. I poured him a beer and stole the first frothy sip, feeling for a moment that everything would be okay no matter what secrets were written in my blood.

We'd moved into this house on Marlowe Avenue, right up the street from our duplex, two months after our wedding. The day before Thanksgiving, we sat in our empty living room with our chocolate Lab, Buckeye, a six-pack, and a pizza. We called the house New Marlowe for a few months before it became, simply, home. We painted and repainted every room, planted flowers and evergreen trees, and spent more money than we had fixing twenty years of deferred maintenance. Both of our dads had tried to discourage us from purchasing it, saying it required too much work and reminding us we could get something newer, nicer, and bigger if we moved farther from the city. But we'd already made our decision and set to work building the life we'd been talking about for years.

Getting our house ready for the new baby was tangible work that delivered instant results. It was the best form of distraction, a reminder that hope can ring louder than fear. But then, as we cleared out our past lives and made room for the new life inside of me, Buckeye got sick. Brian and I had bought him from a breeder in Amish Country a month after we'd gotten engaged, right before moving into our duplex. He was only six years old now, so it was hard to admit something serious might be wrong with him. He was slightly off balance at first, like there was stiffness in his back legs. Then he refused to go up and down the stairs. Over the course of a week or two, he had several episodes of being unable to walk and sliding off our couch like a bowl of Jell-O. We took him to the vet, where he was given medication for arthritis.

Brian and I argued over the next few days, because the medicine wasn't helping. He wanted to figure out what to do next, and I wanted to give it more time.

That Saturday night, after building the crib, we drove across town to buy a new rug for Ben's room so we could move his alphabet rug into the nursery. Ben lay on the beautiful showroom beds and played with the fancy wooden toys he ignored at home. Brian and I lounged on the fresh sofas and pretended to hold glasses with our pinkies out.

This shopping trip was a fun distraction from the more serious issues that took up so much of our attention.

When we came home, Buckeye was sleeping on the couch. As we dragged the new rug upstairs, we smelled something off. Rancid and biological. I ran into the bathroom to see if the toilet had backed up, but the floor was clean.

Brian emerged from the baby's room. "Don't go in there." He pulled the door shut behind him. "It looks like a murder scene of dog shit."

I ran downstairs to check on Buckeye, who, on closer inspection, had poop smeared into the fur on his back. I grabbed a washcloth and made a bucket of soapy water to clean him while Ben sobbed next to me. I refilled the bucket and took it upstairs to Brian, who spent the night washing the floor, ceiling, and walls in the formerly happy, empty green room.

While Brian cleaned the freshly painted walls, I gave Ben a bath and read him his books. Ben talked to my stomach and asked to touch my belly button. He called the baby "my baby," meaning his baby, and in the gentlest and most serious of ways, he explained with complete sincerity the things that were important and exciting to our family.

"Baseball, the Ohio State Buckeyes, and WWE, and Spider-Man, well, all superheroes, football, fruit snacks," he whispered. He gave his baby the tiniest, softest kiss. I was embarrassed about my flat belly button and a freckle that had grown much larger as my skin stretched out. Not Ben. I heard Brian scrubbing the walls and hoped the joy we'd felt earlier that day wasn't getting wiped away with each swipe of his sponge.

The next night, Buckeye froze up again. We called Brian's mom to stay with Ben and took Buckeye to the emergency vet. Without control of his body, Buckeye slid between the front seats and the back seat, unable to hop back up. We had orders to call the vet when we arrived. Two medics came out with a rolling exam table, on which they laid his limp ninety-pound body.

A twenty-four-hour emergency vet's office is a desperate place. It was quiet. Brian and I sat in plastic chairs, unable or unwilling to talk, and we waited. The quiet of our wait was broken by the horrifying howls of a dog, somewhere in the back, who was suffering greatly. Brian paced. I was unable to will my pregnant body into any action beyond stillness.

Several minutes after the suffering dog quieted, a vet came out to talk with us.

"Did you hear the howling back there?"

We nodded.

"That was Buckeye."

Brian was stoic. I was in tears immediately.

"You can come back to see him before you go, but we want to keep him overnight."

Buckeye was panting heavily and bared his teeth when I reached to pet him goodbye. He was no longer the gentle giant who slept next to Ben's bassinet and curled up beside us.

The vet called at 8:00 a.m., exactly, for an update. Buckeye had a tumor on his pancreas, keeping his blood sugar dangerously low. We drove back. Brian punched the steering wheel.

I wasn't ready to talk yet, but as the world outside flicked past me like a slideshow, I thought, *Even my dog is a mutant.*

There were no viable treatment options, and a lack of sugar to the brain meant his seizures would continue, his personality unpredictable. The vet left us alone in the exam room with Buckeye, who lay on the cold, white floor. At home, he had dug two dog-size pits in the dirt next to our house, cool spots for him to rest in the summer heat. He dug another next to a juniper we called "the Buckeye tree." He sprawled out on the tile floor in the bathroom and stretched along the exterior walls in the winter. He loved to both play and lie in the snow of our backyard.

We sat on this cold floor, petting Buckeye and telling him how much we loved him. We told ourselves that saying goodbye was the most compassionate option among a short list of dreadful ones. Though we would never be ready, we found the vet and stayed with our boy as the medicine entered his veins and he peacefully went to sleep forever.

When we picked up Ben from day care, he was upset we hadn't told him Buckeye would die and that he hadn't said goodbye. For weeks afterward, he sat on the couch and pointed at us in turn. "You're here. Dad's here. I'm here. Buckeye's not here." And then, "When is he coming back?"

"Baby, he's not coming back." I would try to rub his back, but he scooched away.

"But you're here, Dad's here, and I'm here."

Our floors had no dog hair on them, aside from when we closed a door that typically hung open and found tufts of his straight, dark hair mixed in with cobwebs. But our floors were now filled with crumbs of food.

"Have I always been this messy of a cook?" I asked Brian while chopping broccoli for a stir-fry.

"Yes. But Buckeye's not around to clean up after you."

I played the same CD I'd listened to after Jeff died, crying each morning on the way to work. I found the singer, Lissie, on a local college radio station, and she sang a breakup song that reminded me of the loss my family had experienced. It wasn't just these lyrics, though. So many of her songs made lovers seem like ghosts, ambling in and out of life. This obscure debut album had the unpolished feel of fresh emotions, broken and brassy. I played it on repeat for weeks, greedy for the salty tears it cleansed from me.

I passed Lake Erie during these rides and noticed how the water was different every day. Flat as a mirror, filled with breaking waves, sapphire, topaz, emerald, slate gray, onyx. Jewels I envisioned setting in a straight line before smashing with a hammer, their dust mixing with sand and air. I couldn't imagine not living next to a body of water. The openness to the north signified nothing if not possibility and, at the same time, reminded me that the waves kept rolling, the sun kept rising, day after goddamn day, regardless of what happened to any of us.

NOVEMBER 2007

Suzie

Brian and I had been married just over a year when my mother-in-law called me on the Monday after Thanksgiving. I was sitting in a line of traffic at the end of the highway exit, on my way home from work.

"Tiffany?" Suzie's voice was higher pitched than usual, and I would later think I knew it was bad news with just that single word.

She proceeded with a string of words my brain struggled to process, most importantly the phrase "breast cancer." I didn't want to hear any of it, but that didn't make them any less real. Suzie and I had a special bond. She didn't have a daughter. I didn't have a mother, and we both filled those spaces in each other's lives. Her own mother had died when she was thirty, so she'd raised her two sons without her mom for most of their childhoods. We had a closeness I appreciated, agreeing that other people seemed to have strained relationships with their mothers-in-law or daughters-in-law, but we both felt fortunate.

"I know it's too much to ask," she said, "but can you tell Brian for me? Please?"

There was nothing to say except yes, of course. By this point, I'd started driving again and pulled into a gas station right off the highway. We only talked for a minute, or two at the most. My entire body began to shake. This was the thing about having parents who were still alive: Their deaths loomed as inevitable, unfaced disasters.

Brian talked to Suzie every day. The ease and reliance that existed between them stoked an envy that burned deep in my guts. It was the kind of relationship I remembered my mom having with my grandma: a regular coexistence, a low hum of interconnectedness between holidays and special events. Suzie had raised Brian and his younger brother, Sam, as a mostly single mother since Brian was in middle school. Half their sizes, she still managed to boss them around, giggling at the jokes they pulled on her, and her sons treated her like royalty. She had the exact relationship with her sons I imagined having someday with my own children.

Just a few days earlier, after a catered Thanksgiving at her house, I'd said to Brian that if his family no longer wanted to cook their own meal, we should step in and host. It seemed sacrilegious to eat store-bought foods devoid of memories, but next to the metal gas pump, it dawned on me why Suzie and her sister hadn't cooked. I felt terrible for being so judgmental, for not seeing this as a clue that something was wrong.

I put my left hand on my right forearm and rubbed up and down, trying to calm myself. I needed to be strong for Brian, to show him that no matter what happened, we would be okay. But the thought of losing Suzie, of watching her suffer, of helping Brian face her death and how that grief would affect our fledgling marriage, left me sobbing. I didn't notice the cars lining up around me until a truck honked. I flipped its driver the finger and pulled out of the gas station parking lot. I couldn't believe Suzie was asking me to break this news to Brian, and at the same time, I knew exactly why she couldn't bear to do it herself.

A few weeks later, Brian and I huddled in a waiting room with Sam and their Aunt Caroline while Suzie underwent surgery to remove the tumor. Pathology showed that the cancer was estrogen receptor–positive, so she would take medication to send her into full menopause. There was also a relief that she had tested negative for one of the breast cancer genes, but that news hadn't meant anything to me at the time. She had three rounds of chemo and then radiation.

Each week, I made her a batch of vegetable soup in a big red pot. It reminded me of the slimy meat loaves and batches of bloated pasta people delivered to our house when my mom was sick. Those disgusting meals, thick with pity and tasting like the inside of someone else's Tupperware. But Suzie said the soup was the only thing she could eat during treatment, so feeling helpless in every other way, I kept making it.

Brian would tell me after visiting how hard it was to witness both her baldness and the cotton turban covering it, how much it hurt to look at his mom and only see cancer during this time. Suzie called him a butthead and told him to get over it, half laughing and half telling him to keep his negative energy away from her.

I struggled to support Brian, who I had to admit was radiating a lot of negativity. Yet I knew this way of being. I'd grown up with it. I'd felt it myself, and I remembered my dad's worries, expressed as anger, filling every room he entered for years. For months, I stood by and tried my best to be present for Brian, even when nothing I did made him feel any better. One of the secrets I kept was that I was afraid of who he'd become if Suzie's treatments failed. I feared him turning into his dad, drowning his sorrows with alcohol. I didn't know how we'd survive without a single mother between the both of us.

I felt like a robot, going through the motions of being a supportive daughter-in-law. Because another thought, impossible to voice, toyed with me. Through all of it, Suzie didn't seem that sick. Or sick enough to die, I guess, when I compared her to my mom. She had chemo, slept for a couple of days, went to work, and then repeated this cycle several weeks later. Yes, her hair fell out. Yes, she had yeast infections in her throat and lost weight and the radiation gave her a painful sunburn and she had horrible hot flashes.

Yet through all of it, Suzie seemed so much like herself. So *alive*.

I couldn't say this to Brian. There was no guarantee that her treatment would work. It also felt like a mixture of bad karma and being a shitty person to pontificate on the ways that his mom seemed to be doing well, or at least far better than any cancer patient I'd ever known.

When her treatment was over, Suzie said she never wanted to see another bowl of vegetable soup again. The mixture of laughter and tears that followed her entry into remission was a new experience for me. Brian's family had gone through something and emerged forever scarred but victorious.

While we were celebrating this victory over cancer, we decided there was no reason to keep waiting to start the family we dreamed about. Suddenly, becoming parents seemed like the most logical, most necessary thing we could do. If we wanted children, why would we want to be a single day older than we already were? That was just one day less with them. In a diner that July, eight months after her diagnosis, Brian and I told Suzie she would become a grandmother, and to this day, I don't think I've ever witnessed such pure joy.

SPRING 2012

The Plan

I had a counseling session with Lou scheduled a couple of days before my appointment with Dr. Arenberg to learn my results. I called him to ask if they were in.

"Do you have them?"

"Not yet, but I'll meet with the doctor before your appointment."

"So if we met this week, it's possible that you would know my outcome but not be allowed to tell me?" I circled the date in my calendar with dark, solid lines overlapping each other.

"I suppose so, yes."

"So . . ." I tried to organize my racing thoughts, which felt a step behind Lou's perfectly measured words. "We're either going to need to cancel this appointment or move up the one for my results. I can't see you knowing you have this news about me. I'd spend the whole time searching your face for signs."

We canceled the counseling session. In my heart, as much as I wanted my results, I needed to hope I was negative for just a little while longer. I missed my dog, I was coming up on a year since losing Jeff, and I had a third birthday party to plan for a joyful boy who deserved to be celebrated.

When the day finally came, Brian and I walked into the doctor's office, next to each other but not touching, each protecting ourselves inside our private cocoons. The heat around his body was a force field. I signed my name in tight cursive at the front desk. Raindrops dripped down the dark tinted windowpane, occasionally colliding with each other and creating a satisfying cascade of droplets. I was five months through my pregnancy, and though my abdomen ballooned out more with this baby than it had with Ben, I hadn't gained as much weight as I did the first time around, possibly because I was nervous all the time and not as hungry, or because I had a little boy to keep up with.

Brian's arms were crossed over his chest, and one of his ankles rested on his knee. I wanted him to make eye contact with me, or to reach for my fingers, but he was deep in his own place. I understood this about him, intellectually. Emotionally, I wanted him to exist in this moment only as my support system, but it was too much to ask of one person, and impossible to expect anyway. I folded my hands together over my belly and tried to imagine what he needed from me. The only thing he needed, and the only thing I wanted to give him, was a negative result.

For Brian, this wasn't just a medical moment—it was a potential fracture in the blueprint of the life we'd been carefully constructing. A positive diagnosis would mean more than medical treatment. It would challenge everything we'd planned. Our dreams of raising our family, the careers we were building, the home we were creating—all could be suddenly suspended. He was likely wrestling with fears far beyond the immediate medical reality: Would he be able to support me? How would this change our trajectory?

I carried my hope that my intention to live a stable, solid life with the family I had made with him would be enough. Enough to earn me my negative result, to show us there was a payoff to hard work.

We were called back, and that was when he held out his hand to mine.

Dr. Arenberg sat down with us at a table in the gray room with tissue boxes. We exchanged pleasantries before her face turned serious. "The news isn't what we had hoped for."

Brian gripped the arms on his seat and tilted it backward, away from the table. She said a stream of words about surgeries and screenings and in vitro fertilization if we wanted another baby. She was the teacher from the Charlie Brown cartoons: sound without meaning. All I heard was my heartbeat inside my ears telling me I had failed this test. Until she focused on me, her brown eyes kind and serious. She set her paperwork on the table in front of her. "Your baby is healthy and, today, so are you. This mutation doesn't change anything about who you are." She reached for my hand. "Except your cancer risks."

I pulled my hand into my lap. It felt heavy and cold. I rubbed my palms together, trying to warm them back up. I rested them on my belly, which usually helped calm me down. I willed the baby inside to move or flip, somehow remind me he was still alive. He didn't stir. I heard the doctor's words, and I knew she was expressing kindness, reminding me of my humanity, but it seemed like she was reading a script. Brian placed his hand on my shoulder, the heat from his skin coming through my sweater. I wanted to run from the building, past the parking lot, away from Brian, who I had failed and with whom I could not make eye contact.

Instead, I smiled and told Dr. Arenberg thank you, a perfectly trained people-pleasing idiot.

During the rest of this appointment, Dr. Arenberg sketched out a plan on a piece of light blue paper that sequenced the tests, screens, and surgeries I would need over time. The Plan, as we'd call it afterward, said that I would have a hysterectomy when I was done having kids. The hysterectomy would remove my uterus, cervix, and fallopian tubes. I would have annual colonoscopies and endoscopies in which my entire digestive tract would be scanned for abnormalities, starting six weeks after the baby was born. If there was anything suspicious, it would be removed. Dr. Arenberg said most colon growths take several years to become cancerous. So, annual screenings would literally nip them in the bud. I would have ultrasounds of my pancreas when I was in my mid to late forties. At some point, I'd have another surgery to remove my ovaries as well, most likely around my fortieth birthday, ten years from now.

"I want to keep your ovaries intact as long as possible because they play such a critical role in bone health and hormonal balance," Dr. Arenberg said in a voice that seemed very far away from me.

"What about my kids?" I asked. My entire body felt like it was made of lead as the weight of this burden shifted from being only about my health to theirs. "Do they need to be tested?"

Her face softened, and though I'd never asked about her family, I suddenly believed she was a mother too. "We suggest letting them make that choice for themselves after they turn eighteen."

Brian turned to me. The muscles in his jaw clenched and unclenched, and a new wave of anxiety took over his face. I'd have given anything in that moment to make it all go away, to pull myself from this bad dream that wouldn't shake me loose. But there I was, another link in a family chain I couldn't break and had possibly already added to.

I thought I had prepared myself for this probability and practiced telling myself I was most likely positive. I had red hair and was left-handed, and I'd had polyps removed at a young age. But in the same way you believe you're prepared for someone to be born or to die, you realize you're nowhere close to ready when it happens.

Brian was incredible at the appointment, asking all the right questions. He was so supportive on the way there, on the way home, and throughout the evening as we took care of Ben together. Once we went to bed, though, his fear surfaced. Everything seemed more manageable by the light of day, but alone in the dark with the truth, he hated knowing our son and unborn baby were at risk, and he didn't want to lie to them by withholding information or forcing them to grow up faster than their friends. I proposed telling them only what they needed when the time was right. Maybe simply having a mom who got screening as part of normal life would make the future less scary to them. We both talked that night, but neither one of us was ready, yet, to listen to the other. Our news was too fresh.

As we lay next to each other, I saw that there were going to be good, positive days and darker days—for both of us. This was the rest of our lives. I thought back to our wedding, when we stood in front of everyone we loved and promised to be there for better and for worse, in sickness and in health. We said those words on a day filled with happiness, when this type of news was light-years away, if not impossible entirely. Now, putting these vows to the test, I could hardly bear being the one responsible for this darkness, knowing there was nothing in my power to make it go away. I felt these things, but they were too raw to say out loud.

Brian had frequently talked about his coworker who had genetic testing and got screened every three months. She had beaten three or four different cancers, but each one had been caught very early. She believed testing and screening had saved her life many times. For Brian, having someone he liked and respected share a similar experience became a source of reassurance—living proof that knowledge is power. But I understood: A coworker wasn't your wife.

As I stared at the ceiling that night, I told myself that in each of my baby pictures, wedding photos, happy memories, sad memories, this mutation was present. It was with me when I went to Europe, when I learned to do front flips off the diving board, when I filed my taxes, and stood on a boat with Brian at the bottom of Niagara Falls. Nothing about my body had changed, only now I knew more about what was going on inside it. I placed my hand on my belly and tried to send love to the baby boy I was pregnant with, this miracle baby we would have been too scared to conceive knowing about the gene. Cars kept driving by, their headlights illuminating the corners of our room. When I closed my eyes to put an end to this day and listened to Brian's breath growing heavy, I crawled through a wormhole to a place where my feelings of love for him burst out of me and into a million different directions, filling the air like confetti, or ashes after a volcano.

PART TWO

APRIL 2012

I Have Some News to Share

The day after my appointment, my hands shook as I dialed my dad's number. I could hear the worry in his voice when he answered. I felt the shame of realizing that, as much as I loved my dad, he loved me even more.

He'd also been rebuilding his life over the past two decades. The summer before, he'd remarried, this time to a woman named Debbi who brought out the best in him. He golfed and rode his bike and enjoyed the freedom he hadn't experienced in his youth while he was busy raising kids and taking care of his dying wife. Even worse than hearing Dr. Arenberg deliver the news was the task of telling my family. It was challenging enough to hear those words spoken by someone else, but having to say them myself made it even more real.

My dad, Danny, and Brittany were the only family members I had told about my testing. We all seemed to be on different timelines and paths toward making that decision. If it was up to me, we would have all done it together, but I knew we each had to process in our own ways. I wasn't even sure if they would test, let alone when. I'd prepared what I was going to say to my dad, repeating my lines over and over. "Knowledge is power," I told myself.

When my dad picked up on the second ring, however, all my preparation crumbled. "I have the gene," I blurted out, the words popping like a champagne cork as the tears and snot I'd been holding inside came out. I had wanted to reassure him, but it wasn't until I heard his voice that I realized I was the one who needed reassurance.

He said all the things the doctor said, about the power of prevention. "I wish we'd known what to watch for with your mother." His voice broke.

"I guess this is better than getting sick and being blindsided down the road," I said. "Mom lost a lot of time, not having any clue what was wrong."

"Have you called your sister and brother?"

I shook my head. "I have to call them next."

"Do you want me to call them for you?"

"I think I need to tell them myself." I needed to own this story and my message, to prove that although I was in a dark place, I was working my way toward something better.

Later that week, I had lunch with my sister at the Mediterranean place we both liked by my office. I'd told her my news days earlier. Britt ripped a piece of pita and dragged it through a plate of hummus. I envied the curls that popped out of her messy bun, along her neck and close to her ears.

"Ryan and I weren't even talking about marriage or kids yet, and now this is forcing us to make some decisions we might not be ready to make." She was only twenty-four, and now that we were both living on our own, it was easy for me to forget I had half a decade on her. She was one of the people I felt closest to in the entire world, but today, there seemed to be a distance between us that put me on edge.

"Do you want kids?"

She took a bite of her pita before answering. "I don't not want them, someday. But I don't want them now."

This was one of my favorite places to eat, but nothing tasted right. My mouth was dry, and the sense that I was forcing this situation on her descended upon me. I turned to the window and saw a woman on her cell phone walking her dog. A ghost of the kind of smiling person I used to be.

I wanted my sister to want kids. I wanted my boys to have cousins to play with, but I knew how all-encompassing it was, even when it was wonderful. Ben had been a terrible sleeper, day care was expensive, he got sick hundreds of times. Yet it was easier to complain about the difficult parts than it was to find words for the complex feelings of love I had for him. I craved him and space away from him equally. Part of my desire for another child was because I was certain there was a more joyful version of infancy I had missed out on. There was no way to describe motherhood to someone on the fence. It didn't feel like something other people should weigh in on.

"Ryan said he's willing to have one now, if I want." She rolled her straw wrapper like a joint and unrolled it, working the paper in between her fingers without looking at it. She'd rode the Megabus home from Chicago most weekends to visit Ryan, not telling our dad she was coming into town. When she moved back, it was into Ryan's apartment, quietly, and without seeking approval. In their own way, they were like Brian and me, braiding themselves together into something stronger.

"I'm sorry this all feels forced on you." I picked a piece of wet napkin from the bottom of my glass. "It definitely seems really urgent right now. But I guess we could have found out about this five years ago or five years from now, since it's not actually happening now. Whatever it is, it's been there forever. It's not new. Just new information."

Brittany set her wrapper on the table and sat up straighter. "I mean, I'm not completely sure where I fall with testing from an ethical standpoint."

Here it was. The judgment I feared, amid my misery. "What do you mean?"

"Well . . ." She paused, as though seeking permission to continue. "What right do any of us have to make these kinds of decisions? I'm not even religious, but it feels like trying to play God or something."

What right, indeed. I felt warmth creep up my cheeks and down my neck, as though I'd eaten a chili pepper.

"And what right do I have to suggest you do the same thing I did?" I asked.

"It's not that. I know you're not pushing. Even though you kind of are." She rolled her green-yellow eyes and gave me half a smile. "You made the right choice for you and how you are. I'm not sure I know what that is yet, though. For me."

APRIL 2012

Abandoned

Brian and I took Ben to an outdoor mall in the suburbs, built to resemble an urban neighborhood. I'd received a gift card to a maternity store for Christmas, and as my pregnancy flew by, I realized if I didn't use it soon, I'd end up wasting it. My brother-in-law, Sam, had recently moved into an apartment above the stores, and the plan was that Brian would take Ben to visit while I went shopping. I would call Brian when I was done and meet him by the maternity store; then I would also see Sam's new place.

The shopping was a success. I found a couple of dresses and was happy to have some new clothes I wasn't tired of wearing. I held my bags, waited outside the maternity store, and called Brian. He didn't answer. I called Sam, and he told me Brian had left ten minutes earlier to meet me. I walked to the end of the block and scanned the sidewalks for my family and traffic for our car, but I didn't see either. The sky grew dark with storm clouds, and the wind picked up as the temperature dropped. Goose bumps spread across my skin. I called Brian a few more times and was sent straight to voicemail. For the first couple of minutes, I was fine. A couple of minutes became a quarter of an hour, and the brewing storm moved into my body while my fear morphed into betrayal.

This was the moment Brian had been waiting for: a perfect fragment of time without me. He'd seized this opportunity to leave. Panic gripped my entire body, squeezing my head and my chest so tightly I thought I might suffocate. This was it. Brian was gone. He took Ben to start over with a new woman and make a new family without the genetic mutation and the mental toll of our situation. I walked around the building corner, crouched down next to it, and cried as hard as I ever remembered crying. I was the girl next to the cathedral years earlier, begging God to save my mom. I didn't know whom I could call to help me, whom I trusted enough to share this devastating news with, or if I'd be better off walking the ten miles back home.

While I was weeping in the alleyway, my phone rang.

"Tiff, where are you?" It was Brian's voice. "We've been looking everywhere."

"What's this number?"

"My phone died. A security officer let me use his phone. We can't find you."

I met Brian by the maternity store, as we planned. He apologized for the confusion, thinking the store was over by Banana Republic, not H&M.

When I got in the car, I stared straight ahead, unable to face him or speak. Once we hit the freeway, I exploded, screaming that I hated him and didn't trust him anymore. The windshield wipers struggled to keep up with the pouring rain, each swipe barely clearing the glass. Brian squinted at the road, alternating between telling me to be quiet so he could focus and calling me crazy. He knew exactly what to say to make me even more upset. I yelled so loudly I made Ben cry in the back seat, his face a crumpled red mess.

We pulled into our driveway, but I couldn't lift myself from the car. Brian unbuckled Ben and shot lasers at me from the black holes where his eyes used to be. He cradled Ben's head in his hand like I wanted someone to do for me and slammed the door shut behind them, disappearing into the rain.

I couldn't make myself stop crying or shake the feelings that were coming out. I knew my emotions were overblown for what had happened—this simple miscommunication—but they refused to settle. I thought I may need to go to the hospital.

I sat in the car and stewed, long after they went inside, humiliated and terrified by what I was capable of, all because I thought my husband had abandoned me and my broken gene. Sitting in our car as the rain poured down, I continued to imagine that Brian might take off with Ben and start over. A clean start. I would be left alone with my baby and the rest of our lives to deal with.

My existence was a burden. Somewhere in the midst of building a family, I'd become a fire to the home Brian and I had painstakingly constructed.

Brian, anxious since childhood, masked his fears with humor, but I knew them all: heights, divorce, losing our kids in a crowd, losing me, losing the boys, losing himself in his grief. Now, I wasn't sure if I was the one pulling away or if he was. I imagined running away, preemptively giving him the loss he feared, letting him start over. It would end my worry that he might leave first, giving him the chance to marry someone who didn't need to endure annual colonoscopies, who wasn't paralyzed by every medical notice, who could give him healthy, unmutated children.

I realized as the rain pounded the roof of the car that I had taken my own escape fantasy and projected it onto him. But that fantasy could never be real, because the man in my story—the one who starts over—could never be Brian. He held tightly to the few people he loved.

Brian hadn't done anything wrong, not tonight or in the doctor's office, or anywhere else. I knew this, but I couldn't make myself believe it. I took a breath and felt my lungs push against my ribs. I wondered if my ribs were capable of stabbing a hole through my lungs and how much it would hurt if that happened. Most days I was positive and optimistic and thought that our life would be okay. Not perfect—that fantasy had long been abandoned. But I thought we would be okay. That we would get through this together, somehow. Yet this fear was lurking right underneath.

Brian didn't want to talk to me when I unlatched the door, and I understood why. I crept around the edges of our living room, perched on the steps, and tried to make Ben smile. After collecting myself, I mustered up every ounce of my courage and told him what I thought had happened. He was still cold, but he hugged me. "I'm so sorry," I said, burying my wet face in his shirt.

"You know that's not how I am," he said. "You know breaking up our family is my nightmare."

I knew this from every story about his childhood I'd ever heard. I'd accused him of something that went against the core of who he was. "I'm so sorry," I repeated. I was sorry for screaming at him, for not trusting him. Sorry for the whole night and for this entire situation. Sorry for becoming someone I didn't know anymore and sorry for asking him to keep loving me.

He pulled back and turned toward Ben, who sat on the floor among a mountain of cars and superhero figures. "You know I finish what I start, right?" Ben looked up. "You know I love you and your mom and I'm not going anywhere, right?"

Ben nodded, and Brian turned to me. "You got that?"

I believed him.

The harder battle was making sure I didn't push him away first.

APRIL 2012

The Puppy

"We can't wait until the baby is born to get a puppy," Brian said, peering up from his laptop. He was camped out on the floor in the upstairs hallway, looking much more studious than I remembered him from graduate school. "If we get one now, we can have it housebroken by the time the baby comes. And if we don't get one now, we'll have to wait until the baby can walk, because having a puppy and a crawler will be too much."

I listened while getting ready in front of the bathroom mirror. While this pregnancy was technically easier than my first one, it was by no means easy. I was no longer throwing up, but I scratched myself all the time, regardless of how much cream I slathered onto my belly. I was tired in a way that felt like it cut straight to my soul, settling deep inside me, as though exhaustion had become a personality trait. I couldn't tell if it was just pregnancy symptoms or something deeper, potentially more serious and long term.

But I did have to laugh at how hard Brian had worked to build this case for a new dog. I didn't need much persuasion. I felt lonely in our quiet house and missed someone cleaning up after me as I made dinner. Having a dog had been the first step Brian and I took together when we decided to make ourselves into a family, and I was eager to fill that absence, however ill equipped I may have been then or now. I also figured I owed him whatever temporary happiness a puppy might bring.

On Easter, my Aunt Andrea sent Brian a text, telling us the breeder they had gotten their golden retriever from had a male puppy available. No pressure! she wrote.

After Ben collected his Easter eggs and started peeling the foil from his chocolates, Brian called about the puppy. "He's twelve weeks, which means he'll be easy to house-train, and I'm on spring break this week, so it's perfect."

The next day, Brian and Ben picked me up from work at lunchtime. An hour later, the puppy napped on my lap. We named him Gus. He didn't erase the loss of Buckeye or fix my DNA, but he showed us that even in the wake of disappointment, life persists. Gus brought the possibility of joy back into our house and became all the fur and puppy cuddles we ever wanted. He joined me on the meandering walks I took throughout our neighborhood every day, not minding that I got slower as my pregnancy progressed. Gus hung out in Ben's room before bedtime, becoming part of our evening routine. He seemed to skip over the typical puppy phase, as though an old dog had been born into a puppy body. He made me feel guilty for how thoroughly we loved him, right from the start.

"I hate to admit this," Brian said, watching Ben play with Gus in the backyard, "but he's such a better dog than Buckeye. I don't love him more, but he's just—"

"So much easier. It's true." I paused to enjoy their play. "Do you think it's because we knew what to do this time? Like we were ready for it?"

Brian squinted, considering. "Isn't it weird he was the last dog to be picked? How did nobody else want him?"

"Was he waiting for us?" I looked up to the sky and pulled my arms behind me, feeling all the muscles in my body stretch. The invisible strings binding me loosened the tiniest bit.

APRIL 2012

Opening

A few months after Jeff died, my grandma moved out of her two-story hundred-year-old house into my Aunt Jenny and Uncle Pat's ranch a few miles away. A week after bringing Gus home, we sat in their front room with the television muted, and I shared my news with them. My mom's older brother, Bernie, and his wife, Donna, were there too, squeezing next to each other on the sofa. Two small dogs made their rounds before one settled in my grandma's lap and the other on Pat's shoulder, like a furry parrot.

I felt bad for not telling them sooner I'd had my blood drawn, like this conversation should have been shared in snippets instead of all at once. But I had thought the news would be easier to share when it had an ending—either positive or negative.

I had received the news of my mutation six days before the first anniversary of Jeff's death. It was now eight days later. Though I hadn't planned the timing, our awareness of that date made it all feel like a tender wound, still healing. Grief seemed to exist on a loop, circling back to remind me how little time had passed.

I thought about how my Grandpa Mitchell had died almost exactly one year before my mom. My sister used to sit on his lap and count out his pills from a plastic case with the days of the week printed on it. The day he died, my mom told me the news right before taking me to gymnastics class. I asked if I should stay home, but she insisted I go. She lived just 367 days longer than her dad. Only as an adult could I comprehend how awful that year must have been—both of them fighting cancer at the same time. Then Jeff got sick. Knowing what we knew now, it seemed naive to have blamed it all on bad luck.

My grandma reached for my hand. "Your grandpa, he wouldn't have been able to handle knowing he passed this on or seeing Julie the way she was at the end. It's a blessing he went before she got that sick." Tears filmed her eyes. "We still have the three of you."

"I know," I said. "And we still have each of you." I gave her palm a squeeze. I didn't want to pressure anyone into getting tested, but I was curious to know if they were considering it, and I felt a sense of urgency to share what I'd learned. I wanted them to understand that screening protocols were different for Lynch patients—more frequent, covering more than colonoscopies—and it was important to me that Jeff's legacy created a positive outcome related to cancer. At the same time, I'd just lived through some of the hardest months of my life, and I knew what a toll it might take. There were two sides to testing, this much I knew. One was the cold, immutable facts of the results. The other was what those facts activated emotionally, which had nearly been my undoing.

I hoped by sharing my news, I was opening a door for them to walk through if they were ready. As hard as the last couple of months had been, I was finding glimmers of relief in realizing I could make decisions proactively instead of worrying about being blindsided by a cancer diagnosis.

I also knew this was a private choice, something each of them would need to make within their own hearts. I couldn't know what kept them up at night or the specific fears they carried. At the same time, I couldn't imagine this happening to one of them, especially if it could be prevented. I hated the idea of my grandma burying another child or watching my aunt or uncle fight the same battle Jeff and my mom had lost. I wished they would allow me to demystify the testing process and show them that even if the news wasn't what they hoped for, they wouldn't be alone.

MAY 2012

A Decision

Brian and I stood in our driveway, watching Ben climb up the ladder of his play set. It was another plastic monstrosity I swore I'd never have, earning its keep. The baby inside me never stopped moving, and I imagined him one day trying to keep up with his older brother.

"When do you think you'll have the surgery?" Brian asked. Ben slid down the red slide, caught himself from falling, and ran to climb back up.

The yard was in full bloom, with a lilac bush next to the garage. The puppy sniffed around the lawn, and if we were talking about anything else, it seemed like this would have been a picture-perfect moment.

I felt my throat grow thick and bit down on my lip. "I thought we already talked about this."

"You keep saying things like 'soon,' but that doesn't help me schedule my time off work to be with you."

"I told you, I'll have it as soon as I'm allowed." I wanted this surgery somewhere between the day I gave birth and never. It was among the most crucial elements of the Plan, something that felt nonnegotiable, but the geneticist insisted it was up to me to decide when we were done having children.

"Are you sure you want to have it when the baby's still so young?"

"Fine, I'll wait to have it."

Ben's attention flickered toward us. Since my outburst in the car, I'd worked harder than usual to calibrate my emotional state around him. I gave him a thumbs-up.

"Look, it's your decision. I'm just asking." Brian moved toward the lilac bush, like he was curious about something in the leaves. He was probably just trying to get away from me.

Ben slid to the bottom of the slide and shoved his finger into the dirt.

"None of this is my decision. None of this is what I asked for." I put my hand on what I was convinced was the baby's butt. It fit into my hand like a teacup or a clementine, a talisman that made me feel safe. I didn't realize how much of my adulthood would be spent nurturing the child I used to be, how much energy I would pour into trying to make things right for someone I no longer was. If I could give my own children a solid, peaceful childhood—the life I wished I'd had—then maybe I would make up for everything that had broken down in mine.

"Nobody will be mad at you if you give yourself a break and take some time to think about this." Brian stepped back toward me.

"I don't want more time to think about it." I felt the thickness in my throat expanding, like my tongue was bread rising, and the sting of tears I didn't want Ben to see. "All I do is think about this, you know? I just want to get it over with. If something happened to me that we knew might happen and should have been prevented, I wouldn't be able to face you guys." I pulled my cardigan tight across my chest.

"What do you think about the IVF thing?" The geneticist had told us we could pursue in vitro fertilization if we wanted, in which they would test embryos for Lynch syndrome and only implant ones without the mutation.

I shook my head. "I can't give nonexistent future kids better odds than the ones we have." Ben slowly pulled himself up the slide. When he reached the top, he slid back down on his belly, feet first.

"You don't have to rush it," Brian said. "She said you can wait until you know you're done having kids."

"How does anybody know that anyway? We may have only ever wanted two kids, and I'm fine with only boys, but now it's this whole thing. Plan your whole life right now. I don't think I could live with this hanging over me. And then what? I shortchange the baby because I start trying to get pregnant right away, just to prove I can? And before I know it, Ben's childhood is over and I've spent the whole time obsessing over when or if to have another one instead of focusing on the kids we have?"

Brian smiled, as though he were conducting group therapy and I was one of his students he'd gotten to share something they'd been sitting on. I hated it when he was able to trick me with his professional skills, but I had to admire him for it at the same time.

"Are you okay with two kids?" I asked, suddenly aware that he had feelings on this subject I hadn't been considering. Brian had his own childhood he was trying to make up for, his own pressure he put on himself to be the kind of dad he and his younger brother had needed, his own vision for what constituted a good childhood.

He shrugged and looked over at Ben. "It was just boys in my house growing up. I guess I've been a little curious about what a girl would be like. Not that I'd know what to do with one."

"The thing I love about being one of three," I said, "is that when Danny or Brittany are bugging me, I can always talk about it with the other one. You and Sam just call your poor mom all the time."

"You know how many people I know who tried for a girl and ended up with three boys anyway?" Brian asked.

I counted off a few families, including one set of his cousins. "I mean, if we stop now, we'll definitely never have a daughter. Would you be okay with that?"

Brian touched my belly. "I'd be okay. Would you?" He seemed wistful in the same way I felt.

I'd tamped down some disappointment both times the ultrasound techs had announced, "It's a boy!" From as far back as my trip to Virginia when my aunt hid the baby-name book in my suitcase, I'd been imagining the daughter I'd have one day. But what was adulthood but the constant realignment of dreams and reality? The crux of each of our dreams hinged on both parents being alive and in love, and when I boiled it down to that, there was no option but to do everything in my power to be both of those things.

"There was never a guarantee we'd have a girl anyway," I said. There were no guarantees about anything.

JULY 2012

Brothers

Over the next couple of months, my body and its mutated MSH6 gene continued to grow and ultimately delivered a vital, blond boy on his due date in only two pushes. We named him Andrew, and we loved him instantly.

Andy was born in the middle of the night. The next afternoon, my mother-in-law, Suzie, brought Ben to visit us. He walked into my hospital room wearing the Spider-Man outfit we'd bought him the day before, when I'd taken him to the mall to try to kick-start the weeks of middling contractions I'd had into something stronger. At the mall, we'd taken pictures in a photo booth, snapping what we guessed would be our last pictures as a family of three.

After we went home, I insisted on walking to my forty-week doctor's appointment, where I convinced the midwife to sweep my membranes. I'd been three centimeters dilated for weeks at this point, walking around like a boiling cyst about to burst.

When Ben finally met his baby brother, the one he'd spent so much time talking to through my skin, he was quiet, tentative to let go of Suzie's hand. I cradled his delicate, red-faced brother and invited the new big brother onto the bed with me. Ben looked like a giant, peering at his brother with the same awe and confusion I felt myself. After

I placed Andy in his lap, Ben relaxed. He told us about going to the playground and how Grandma let him eat doughnuts for breakfast and fast food the night before. Ben was meeting his brother, but Brian and I also saw our sons, our family, whole, for the first time. Suzie and Ben stayed for hours, doing nothing and everything.

AUGUST 2012

The Magazine

A women's health magazine I never subscribed to kept showing up in the mail. Within its pages, smiling, sweatless women demonstrated exercises in spotless, uncluttered homes. When Andy was two weeks old, napping in a portable bassinet, I found myself unable to focus on anything more demanding than glossy magazine articles. So I decided to follow along, one slow, painful move at a time. Plank, squat, something on my back while kicking my legs. I was supposed to repeat each sequence three to five times. My midsection burned. The magazine told me that was my core. I breathed heavily and I wanted to stop, but these simple moves showed me not only how weak I was but how much stronger I could become.

I promised myself I would do one workout from the magazine every day. I worried I would start bleeding again, but the blood draining from me was only brown, old, and leftover. At first, I was embarrassed by my weakness. I also felt ridiculous exercising in the middle of our living room, putting myself on display for Brian and Ben, but it was the only space I had. I gained strength, though, and more quickly than I expected, with each move becoming easier as the weeks passed. I looked forward to each new magazine and hoped they would keep showing up.

One evening after Andy was asleep, I told Brian I was going for a walk. I unearthed my old tennis shoes, laced them tight, and closed the door behind me. My breasts felt heavy and my stomach squishy, but I only had one life and one body, so I jogged down the driveway to the sidewalk. From our house, I jogged to the street corner, about a quarter of a mile. My legs and lungs felt like I'd poured acid on them. I didn't want my neighbors to see me, so I walked to the next block. When I hit the street behind our house, I picked a tree, three houses down. *Just run to the tree.* I ran to the tree; then I walked to the light pole. From the light pole, I ran to the third driveway, then walked to a fire hydrant. I picked destinations a couple of houses apart and ran, then walked, then ran, then walked for my next quarter of a mile. Finally, I made it home, jogging a total distance of half a mile, feeling like I'd been gone forever.

When I came up the stairs to the kitchen, the clock on the stove told me it had been twelve minutes. I realized that for the past twelve minutes, I hadn't thought about cancer or my looming hysterectomy. I hadn't worried about the colonoscopy scheduled for a few weeks out. Instead of worrying about my entire future, I worried only about getting from the oak tree to the fire hydrant.

This feeling of turning off my brain became a drug, giving me a break from my parallel existence. Outwardly, I made healthy food, exercised, snuggled with Andy, played with Ben, and stayed positive for Brian. Inwardly, I worried I was already too late. Cancer cells were multiplying inside me as I inched closer to my mom's age when she died, three weeks shy of her thirty-first birthday. My thirty-first birthday would be on New Year's Eve, a few months away.

As my uterus contracted back to being the size of a pear instead of a watermelon, I imagined it becoming gray and black, like the pictures we saw of smokers' lungs in elementary school. To offset my fear, I exercised harder, reasoning without reason that if I was able to hold a plank for sixty seconds and run two miles, then I probably didn't have cancer. I found a jogging stroller at a yard sale and strapped Ben into it, zigzagging the streets throughout my neighborhood, running away from and toward the same thing.

AUGUST 2012

The *Goodtime*

Andy was snug in a baby carrier, his cheek pressed against my chest. I loved the feel of his warm sleeping face against my skin, the dampness where we touched. Brian was home for the summer, a perk of his teaching schedule. He held Ben's hand as we boarded the *Goodtime*, a tour boat that cruised Lake Erie and the Cuyahoga River. The lakefront was the same one I'd visited during the rib cook-off almost twenty years earlier, though the architecture along the shoreline had changed.

"It's hard to believe we've never done this before, isn't it?" I said, excited for our mini adventure. After the endless grind of day care drop-offs and pickups, community meetings, night school, and doctors' appointments, these uninterrupted days together felt like a gift. Knowing this was my last maternity leave made it even more precious. I didn't mind waking in the night to feed Andy. Instead of groaning every time he woke up, I etched his sea creature fingers and cloudy blue eyes into my memory. The sweetness I had hoped for when we were trying to conceive was more delicious than I imagined.

As we floated down the river, a voice over a loudspeaker narrated Cleveland's industrial history, pointing out the steel mills, the architects who designed the skyline, and bits of local trivia. From the water, the buildings seemed smaller than they were from the sidewalk. Ben sat on Brian's lap and pointed at everything, his curious mind wanting names and stories to go with the sights. As we entered Lake Erie and passed the Cleveland Browns Stadium and the Rock & Roll Hall of Fame, I had a fleeting thought that someday Lynch syndrome wouldn't be the first thing I thought about in the morning, that maybe if my life were a guitar, Lynch could become only one string instead of my entire song.

SEPTEMBER 2012

A Peek Inside

As I savored my days with baby Andy, I tried to ignore my upcoming colonoscopy and endoscopy until it was time. That moment came when I walked into the pharmacy and picked up a brown paper bag containing a gallon-size plastic container, its bottom coated with various powders. The directions said to fill with water and place in the refrigerator for a day. My stomach retched at the thought of consuming so much of this salty medicinal liquid. I knew from experience that each cup became harder to swallow.

The colonoscopy itself would be the easy part. It was the day before I had to mentally prepare for. The liquid diet would leave me hungry, and it would be a battle to get enough fluids to produce breast milk and stay hydrated myself. There was also the potential of waking up to bad news. My last colonoscopy had been six years earlier, a few months before our wedding, and an adenoma, or noncancerous polyp, had been removed. I tried to ignore this worry by cleaning out Ben's dresser and vacuuming the corners of his room, changing his sheets, reorganizing Andy's diaper station, and making sure there were only matching socks in my own drawer. I wiped down the refrigerator inside and out and took the dog for a walk. I tried not to talk, because when I did, I felt hurtful words forming inside my mouth, a nervous fight brewing inside the body I couldn't escape. It was a day to survive, not to enjoy, like the long, weary day of travel it takes to get to a foreign country.

I stocked up on clear beverages and sent Brian out to get my favorite matzo ball soup, minus everything but the broth. He entertained Ben while I set my clock, drinking eight ounces from my gallon at a time, one cup every ten minutes until I wanted to prick my belly button with a pin to release the air building up inside.

I fell asleep on the couch, not wanting to wake Brian every time I got up to use the bathroom. He heard me anyway and came downstairs to check if I was okay. How awful was I for wanting to be invisible, resenting his kindness for being more attention than I could handle—yet knowing I'd resent him more if he didn't offer it.

With confirmation that the laxative was safe for breastfeeding, I fed Andy overnight, agitation flickering beneath my freckles. There it was, a shadow glimpse into those last years with my mom, and the shame of understanding how much our daily needs had burdened her. Constant hunger, fighting, messes to clean, homework to help with, the overwhelming love coupled with an unrelenting need for care—all while launching her new career as an intensive care nurse, sustaining her marriage, and facing the god-awful fate we all feared from her first screams inside the car.

I imagined all she wished to say, or do, or see. If she knew she had only thirty more nights with us, would she have crawled into our sheets or given us ice cream for breakfast while we watched the sun rise? Would she have let us skip school and lie in the sand, let the waves roll over us? Were my mom's final months on morphine meant as much to calm her raging, angry heart as to ease the pain that tore through her body like a hurricane?

Caring for newborn Andy gave me another glimpse into my mom's life as a mother, this time as she crept toward her death. This was a penance too. For the entire length of my pregnancy, my mom had been a harbinger instead of a person, with a fate I was desperate to avoid. I couldn't enjoy those milky midnight moments without honoring her losses.

I felt a friendship developing between us as well. We were the same age now, and I could see my mom as someone who had an entire life and existence separate from her cancer. For so many years, I'd seen her as a patient, not a person. But as I struggled to integrate my genetics into the rest of my life, as opposed to letting it define me, I began to imagine what my mom must have felt as she lost her ability to use her body the way she always had. Where I saw only a sick person, she was still herself.

What might I have said if I was drinking coffee at her kitchen table while her children hung from the swing set? I wished I could have told her she was doing a great job managing such a terrible illness. I would have asked her what I could bring for dinner and given her plastic bottles of bubbles to make her baths more soothing. Maybe she would have told me she was scared. Or remarked how horribly ironic it was that she worked in the ICU for two years before becoming a patient there herself. Maybe we would have laughed together more, or she would have offered to teach me how to sew.

What solace might I have offered her? How would Andy's tiny head have nestled against her chest? What outfits would she have made for him? Instead of turning these thoughts off, I stayed with them, imagining I was offering her the friendship we never had the chance to develop. I began to wonder if these thoughts were her spirit, quietly embedding itself within me, her way of staying alive.

I woke early the next day, if I slept at all. I swallowed the second half of my superpowered laxative and sat in the hottest tolerable bath as I waited for the bubbles building in my belly to work their magic.

When Brian and I arrived at the hospital, my dad was already in the waiting room. Shortly after checking in, I was taken back into pre-op, leaving them together and Brian holding a buzzer, as though he were waiting for his table at a chain restaurant. I changed into a gown, and a nurse came in to ask me a bunch of questions and take my blood pressure before inserting an IV into my right arm. She confirmed that I was scheduled for both an upper endoscopy and colonoscopy that day. She asked if I wanted a blanket before she left, and I said no, thank you. A book sat unopened on my lap. Instead, I thought about an article that said the human body regrows itself every seven years or so. I wondered how much of my own body had regenerated during that time and if my DNA was fixing itself or continuing to print bad copies. I regretted having declined the blanket.

After nearly an hour, a nurse came to wheel my bed down to the procedure room. The doctor performing my scopes reminded me of the older activist women I worked with. She had short curly hair and a lot of energy. I pictured her caring for a community garden or hosting a foreign exchange student.

"I always start at the bottom. But don't worry—I use different tubes." She laughed at her own joke. I wanted to be a good sport and laugh with her, but my face felt stiff. I gave her my best attempt at a smile instead.

"Don't worry." She shifted her bedside manner. "I'm what they call high frequency. If there's anything in there, we'll get it out."

The medicine for colonoscopies is not full anesthesia. It's called "twilight sleep," meaning the doctor can say, "Tiffany, I need you to shift a little to your left," and you can hear her, while not caring at all that there is a six-foot tube inserted into your anus. I heard them chatting but didn't pay any attention at all to what they said, blissed out.

I woke up in recovery, confused by the bright lights. Brian and my dad walked back and stood, both with their arms crossed as they listened to the doctor. I heard her words, but they flowed in and out of my head like water in a colander. I closed my eyes.

"No, Tiffany," the nurse said. "We need you to stay up now."

They kept talking, and I dutifully drank the cup of ginger ale the nurse had brought me. I felt my stomach rumble to life.

"How did it go?" I asked Brian, my voice jagged. "And what's wrong?" I put my hand to my throat.

"You did such a good job, babe," Brian whispered as he helped me get dressed. "The doctor removed one benign polyp from your esophagus, but she says you're perfect."

That day, we unknowingly started a ritual. After each colonoscopy, he tells me how the procedure went while I carefully put on the coziest clothes I own. By the time we reach the car, I've forgotten the details and ask, "How did it go?" He patiently repeats that they didn't find anything suspicious, that I did great. At home, he toasts me a bagel before I lie down in our bed, cocooned under our down comforter. I ask him again, "How did it go?" and he tells me, once more, how well I did. I sleep for a couple of hours, my best nap of the year.

SEPTEMBER 2012

Negative

I opened the refrigerator, wishing the odds and ends inside would magically assemble themselves into Ben's breakfast. The cool air brushed my face, and I stood there longer than necessary. Late summer in Cleveland was more humid than hot, leaving the wood floors and dining room table perpetually sticky, like the house itself was sweating. I scrambled some eggs, waiting for my phone to ring. My sister had gone ahead with her testing after all, and her appointment had started twenty minutes earlier.

From the living room, I heard Ben reciting lines from *Toy Story*, as though Buzz Lightyear and Woody had implanted themselves in his mind.

I heard his footsteps coming into the kitchen. "Did you name Andy after Woody's friend?"

I turned toward him. How was it possible that when I saw his shaggy blond hair and his bright white chest sitting above his gray shorts, I felt like I missed him?

"We did not, actually, name your brother after that Andy." I handed him a strawberry. "When did you get so big?"

He lifted his fingers to his chin, as he seriously considered the question. "I guess every day?" He bit into his strawberry. His teeth turned red, and though I knew it was the fruit, it worried me for a moment as I imagined his mouth filling with blood. He went back to his movie, where I heard Woody chasing after the moving truck.

It was taking too long for my phone to ring. No missed calls. A few months earlier, Danny had undergone testing and turned out to be positive too. Danny, who had never had a polyp but did have Crohn's, shared the mutation with me. Brittany, like me, had occasional polyps. Mathematically speaking, there was only a 12.5 percent chance that all three of us had inherited the mutation. Danny never told us he was getting tested and then shared his results afterward, as matter-of-fact as if he were telling us the score of the Browns game.

After an hour, I called Brittany.

"Hey, did you get my text?" There was noise in the background.

"No, where are you?"

"We're at breakfast." Her voice was filled with lightness. "I was negative."

I closed my eyes. Every color flashed behind my eyelids. Of course I wanted her to be negative. But the ugliest envy I ever felt slithered through me. It didn't make sense. I should have felt happy for her. If not happy, then at least relieved. I leaned over the counter's edge and pushed my forehead into the corner. I lifted my head up and brought it back down, hard, feeling the countertop press against my skull. I couldn't wake the baby or draw Ben's attention to the kitchen. I silently jammed my head against the counter, a kaleidoscope spinning within me until I was able to stand upright again.

The best way I can describe how much I love having a sister is the jealousy I feel toward people who have more than one. When I found out the baby who would become Ben was a boy, one of my first thoughts was, *I'll have to have at least three if I want sisters.* Learning Andy was a boy dispelled the fantasy I would ever have a pair of sisters. When Brittany's genetic test came back negative, my happiness for her was counterbalanced by the knowledge that we would not go through this together. I would be alone in assessing the risks for myself without someone making similar decisions alongside me. She won the coin toss and I did not.

My logical brain knew I didn't want her to be at risk. I already had a family and a career path I was happy to be on. She was still building so much of her life. But that didn't mean I felt rationally about it.

Brittany would never need to worry about her DNA mutating on itself. She would keep her reproductive organs and never sit in a genetic counselor's office with her young adult children, listening to the results of their tests. She would never have to wonder if her perfect baby would become an adult who could lose an early battle to cancer.

After several minutes, I opened the kitchen door and went outside onto the new deck Brian had built that summer. Sitting on the back steps, I looked over the yard, at the trees and shrubs Brian planted and watered with such care. I saw the plastic swing set, the T-ball tee, the Wiffle balls, the tiny basketball hoop. The grass glimmered beneath the morning sun. I'd lost the big coin toss, but it suddenly seemed like I'd won so many others.

Birds sang from our bushes, unburdened by their mortality. In their songs, I heard the music of being alive, not the fear of being eaten by a coyote or a hawk. I placed my fingers on my neck beneath my jaw and felt its comforting pulse. My own heart was just as ignorant, thumping away one precious beat at a time.

OCTOBER 2012

Standing Guard

I lugged Andy's car seat through the maze of hallways at the same hospital Jeff had died in and where my blood had pulsed into glass vials six months earlier. Dr. McGinnis was the surgeon recommended by the geneticist, a specialist in treating women with hereditary gynecological cancers. As the car seat grew too heavy in one arm, I shifted it to the other, proud of my ability to multitask: I was getting exercise at the same time I was planning my hysterectomy. Who said women couldn't do it all?

Brian had gone back to work several weeks earlier, and I promised him I could manage the trip to the doctor on my own. In fact, I needed to do this one on my own. The ambivalence I felt about this pending surgery tugged at me. I wasn't worried about the surgery itself, but about the recovery and what it meant to be truly closing the door on having any more children.

I pressed the elevator button and stepped into the empty vault. I set the car seat down and stretched out my arms and fingers. My wrists cracked as I moved them in circles, and I wished I hadn't been so preoccupied with getting to my appointment that I'd forgotten to bring the stroller to snap the car seat into.

Dr. McGinnis had round glasses, round cheeks, and a quick smile. It took a moment to register that this normal-looking man, who reminded me of any number of my neighbors or day care dads, was qualified to slice women open, remove their cancers, and prescribe their chemotherapy regimens. Until he entered the room, I didn't realize I was expecting a crotchety curmudgeon to be the kind of person who made a living doing this work.

We shook hands, and he sat on a rolling stool to review my chart. I tilted the car seat back and forth with my toes an inch at a time, making sure Andy continued to sleep on the floor next to me. His birdlike fingers gripped a strap over his chest. I wondered what he was dreaming about.

"So, when are you thinking about having the surgery?" Dr. McGinnis glanced at Andy. "Congratulations, by the way. He's beautiful."

"I guess as soon as you'll let me?" My voice rose at the end of this question, almost crying, but not quite.

"Around three months postpartum, your uterus should be back to its regular size, which makes the surgery much easier for both of us. Anytime after that would work."

"Well . . ." I swallowed and took a deep breath. "I really want to keep nursing him. Would I have to stop when I have surgery?"

He shook his head. "Nope. Believe it or not, your uterus doesn't have any connection to the hormones you need to continue breastfeeding. If you're done having babies, and that choice remains up to you, your uterus's work is done."

The tears that had been building broke their invisible dam when he said that. I'd been hoping, I now realized, that breastfeeding would give me a few more months, maybe a year. At the same time, I was once again in awe of the human body, each organ and vessel so specifically designed to carry out their particular tasks.

"Let's keep your ovaries for now," he said, reaffirming the Plan. "There are a lot of tests we can run on your ovaries, but to be honest, there are a lot of false positives. If you go poking around for things to be wrong with them, you'll end up having them removed sooner than later."

I appreciated his levelheadedness, and while I wasn't excited to have the surgery, I was looking forward to having it behind me. I had four weeks to go.

Several days before surgery, an ultrasound showed my uterus was back to normal, making it easier to remove. I managed my trepidation by following the Plan, or what I'd come to think of as "the opposite of suicide." In order to carry out the Plan, I only had to physically show up for a series of appointments. I didn't have to want the hysterectomy, I just had to be at the hospital on the right date at the right time, and the doctors would take it from there. I didn't have to connect emotionally with the Plan, I only had to cross items off the list.

Surgery would be my first night away from Andy. My mother-in-law would stay at our house overnight. For weeks, I'd been growing my freezer stash of breast milk. I worried constantly: about being away, about something happening to me in surgery, about the fragile balance of going back to work. I felt out of control, a spectator in my own life. Pumping milk and saving it for later was something I could control, a specific action that was both productive and useful.

The sky turned pink as I rechecked my overnight bag and recounted the bottles of milk in the fridge. Ben still wore the Spider-Man pajamas, which we washed nearly every day. Even though it was my first night away from Andy, it was Ben who made my chest constrict when we said goodbye. He hung on me like the actual Spider-Man gripping the side of a skyscraper and promised to be home when we came back. We hadn't told him why we were leaving, but I imagined our nervous energies clinging to him like wet sand. I hoped that once we were on the other side of surgery, I could spend more time with him again, doing the loving, emotional work of mothering instead of just the daily things that needed doing.

When you go to the hospital to have a baby, you carry feelings of excitement and anticipation. The bag Brian lifted from my shoulder was packed with dread, sadness, and shame. In the car, we listened to sports radio as the city skyline gave way to the industrial buildings and warehouses on the road in between downtown and University Circle.

Once again, I left my dad and Brian in a waiting room. One more time, they told me they loved me, they were proud of me, they'd be here when it was over.

The cuff on my arm in the preoperative unit delivered my first-ever high blood pressure reading, and then my second. I silently said thank you and then goodbye to my uterus and told her it wasn't her fault. I squeezed my eyes shut when I pictured the children I'd never have, the perfect babies I might not want if they weren't impossibilities. My heart beat furiously. The nurses gave me a sedative and told me to ask Dr. McGinnis about race cars when I went into the operating chamber. They laughed about his expensive and dangerous stress-relieving hobby, just another day in the office. They checked my tubes and cords, rechecked the IV in my wrist, touched my feet, and decided to put socks on them. I closed my eyes, pretending to be anywhere but there. The operating room was bright white and so cold and could have been any place in the world. I did ask about race cars but was asleep before I heard an answer.

When I woke up from surgery, the news was positive. My ovaries were beautiful, my uterus was pink and perfectly healthy. Everything had gone so smoothly that they had time for a quick scan of my nearby internal organs—all of which appeared to be normal.

Planned hysterectomies in the twenty-first century are minimally invasive, with surgical tools inserted through the belly button and four careful quarter-inch incisions around the abdomen where tiny cameras are placed, allowing the team to see what's happening inside. My uterus, cervix, and fallopian tubes were removed vaginally, as though I'd given birth to the pieces of my body that had twice allowed me to give birth in the first place.

As the day progressed and my medicines wore off, I felt sore in the most unexpected places. My shoulders throbbed, and my inner thighs felt like I had completed the workout of my life.

"They compress you, trying to make the birth canal as short as possible by pulling your legs up towards your head," my nurse explained. "And your shoulders are sore because your abdomen was filled up with air, giving them room to work. No other way for the air to escape, other than floating up. It should go away in a couple of days." She also drained the bag holding my urine, since I was to be on a catheter until the next day.

After a half hour or so, I had the overwhelming urge to pee. "Brian, call the nurse!" I said. "Is this normal?" She came back and fiddled with the catheter bag so the urine was higher than the tubes that drained it away. Thirty minutes later, the feeling came back. The nurse returned and readjusted the bag. Brian watched, and when the bag filled up the next time, he emptied the orange urine himself. He adjusted that bag all day and all night. My husband, my nurse.

Nurses came into my room every hour, checking my pulse and blood pressure. "You must be a runner. Your heart is very efficient."

I smiled modestly but beamed inside. "I wouldn't say that I'm a runner, but I have been running sometimes."

I went back to sleep.

Only to be jolted awake by a rush of people crowding around my bed, the machines buzzing urgently—something was wrong. "We need you to wake up, Tiffany." A woman's voice was loud in my ear.

I felt hands on the sides of my head. Brian's voice. "Tiff, come on," he said. "Her blood pressure is always on the low side," he said.

"Not this low," someone else said.

I wanted to keep sleeping. I was so tired, so comfy. I wished they would leave me be, but they hummed around me, propped me upright, and added fluids to my IV. When they finally left, and the machines went back to their steady, rhythmic chirps, Brian pulled his chair close to my bed. Watching my postsurgical blood pressure all night, Brian stood guard, part hawk, part angel.

NOVEMBER 2012

Work/Life

Four weeks later, I returned to work. Sixteen weeks had passed since Andy was born. Every cell in my body felt different, but the moment I pushed open the door and started up the stairs, the paint in the stairwell smelled the same. The plants by the entryway were unchanged. The kitchen still reeked of microwaved lunches. My computer password still worked. My desk was dusty, but there was a bouquet of flowers on it and a card welcoming me back. Stacks of paper with my handwriting—notes and to-do lists—waited for me, full of tasks I barely remembered writing down. I hoped my team had taken care of all of it in my absence and learned, quickly, that most of it remained for me to pick back up.

My medical leave had given me two additional weeks at home, but I'd outgrown the liminal stage I was living in. As much as I loved being home with Andy, I was itchy to return to my normal life. The first couple of days after surgery had been painful. Every piece of me felt tender and raw, both inside and out. But I healed quickly. After two weeks of tentative walks around our neighborhood, I laced up my running sneakers, strapped Ben into the jogger, clipped a leash onto Gus's collar, and headed out. Brian cautioned me to be careful. I promised him I would be, but I had no intention of living small. My entire life was built on being careful. He could be careful—I would be strong. Stronger than this mutation and stronger than the sad cards I received in the mail and stronger than the pitying looks I felt from my family and friends and stronger than the self-doubt that crept into every inch of my life. I'd been behaving like a sick person for the past several months, but I was healthy and was ready to live as such.

I felt some peace in leaving Andy with my Uncle Pat's sisters, the same women who cared for Ben as a baby and who made me toast the morning after my mom died. The first time I had left Ben for work, I cried the entire way, but with Andy, I felt triumphant. I survived testing and surgery. I was ready to tackle my project list, to get lost in the search for artists and designers, to craft grant proposals and attend community meetings. I was ready to get outside of my own mind and rejoin the world as I had known it before.

I loved my work—transforming fledgling ideas into tangible projects for Clevelanders to enjoy. But I felt disoriented as I moved through my meetings on those first days back, redundant and slow, a viscous liquid trying to determine my shape. Twice a day, I locked myself in the computer closet to pump, holding one of Andy's socks to my nose and tricking my breasts into letting down their milk.

My world narrowed down to essentials: work, children, exercise, children, food, children, house, children, husband, children. Brian was nearly done with his master's and teaching licensure and still in night school. I wasn't unhappy, exactly, but I was in survival mode, learning our new routine and grasping at fleeting wisps of the gratitude I wanted to feel.

Somewhere in the middle of this, I saw a rat run across the kitchen floor and disappear behind the radiator.

"Brian!" I screamed, dropping to the floor, searching for proof that my eyes hadn't betrayed me.

After explaining what I'd seen, he carried a flashlight up from the basement and lay on his stomach, shining the light under the radiator and refrigerator. I left the kitchen, unwilling to watch what might unfold. After several minutes, Brian walked into the living room, where I sat on the floor as Andy rolled back and forth across a blanket.

He held a brown oak leaf in his hand. "Is this what you saw?"

I considered the leaf and how it may have looked blowing across the floor, how maybe it was the same size as a rat and possibly the same color. My cheeks grew warm. "I'm so sorry for freaking out. I swear I thought I saw something running."

"I, for one, am glad you didn't actually see anything running." He turned his attention to Ben, who had approximately seven hundred toys scattered across the floor. The wooden pieces of a train set intermingled with cars, superheroes, and LEGOs. "Let's clean this up, okay?"

Ben grabbed a plastic bin off the shelf and dumped its contents onto the rug.

"Benjamin Matthew!" Brian picked Ben up and dropped him on the couch. A flash of anger crossed his face, a searchlight scanning the ground. Ben started to cry. I felt my own flash of something, like the walls of our house were squeezing me and I had nowhere to go.

"The inmates are running the asylum," Brian said after we collapsed into bed that night.

I didn't want to fight, but the words slipped out anyway. "You were too rough with him."

"You just sat there, letting him destroy the house. Someone has to raise our kids." He rolled over, his back to me.

"You think I'm not doing enough?" He'd hit a nerve. I knew I wasn't giving Ben the attention I wanted, but I thought Brian understood I was doing my best.

"It's not that. I'm just so fucking tired," he said.

Guilt hit me hard. I wasn't just trapped in my body or this situation. Brian was too. He didn't share my DNA, of course, but he was clinging to the edge of the same abyss. He loved our boys just as much and sought to protect them just as strongly. I reached out and put my hand on his back, feeling his warm skin rising and falling beneath my palm. He was working as hard as I was, maybe even harder, to keep our lives intact. After he spent all day working with other people's children, offering them tools to manage social and emotional problems and breaking up their fights, he had to come home and do it all again. With me. At some point, had I stopped being his partner? Had our home stopped being a refuge?

I suddenly felt how stressful this all was to him, how unfair it was that I hadn't seen this before. Lynch syndrome belonged not only to me, but to my family. I hadn't been strong enough until this moment to see his worries along with my own. In our dark, quiet bedroom, I imagined my hand was a battery and his body was a power source. I closed my eyes and willed myself to pull some energy from him, to lighten his burden as he'd been doing all along for me.

DECEMBER 2012

The Rats

It was four days before Christmas, and the paper sitting on the counter had only one box checked: RATS. It turned out I did know the difference between a rat and a leaf, it's just that rats are smart enough to find places to hide.

Brian walked me through the basement, pointing out where he'd need to fill in the old coal chute and where the exterminator had laid out traps and bait boxes. He showed me their nest, built into the bottom of the empty fish tank, shoved into a forgotten nook near our boiler.

"They found the warmest possible space," he said, shaking his head. "But now, I have something truly horrifying to show you." I didn't know how it could be worse. He placed his hands on my shoulders and steered me to his Man Room, a basement cave built entirely out of plywood. We'd joked that it must have been a shop class project for the previous owner's sons when we moved in. Behind the couch, in another space we never thought about, just on the other side of the wooden wall of the fish tank, was a mound of rat shit.

Andy slept in a carrier on my chest while I put every scrap of food inside our cupboards and bleached every surface of the kitchen. Brian spent the rest of the day crossing items off the exterminator's punch list. We high-fived when he was done. When the boys were in bed, I wrapped presents at the dining room table and listened to the Tears for Fears station on Pandora. I could sleep.

On Christmas morning, Ben crept into our room. "Did Santa come?" His tiny voice was so close to my face that I jumped, startling him in return.

"Come rest for a little while longer. It's still so early." I tried to pull him close to me, missing his little body in my bed. He flopped like a fish until Brian got up.

"I'll go see if he came, okay?" The stairwell glowed pink when he plugged in the tree.

"What do you hope Santa brought you?" I traced Ben's elbow with my fingertip. He'd fallen off the sofa that summer, fracturing his arm near the growth plate. I was grateful for how fast and fully he healed.

"Everything I asked for!" Ben whispered. His excitement was so pure I wanted to stamp this moment into my memory.

"Tiff, I need you," Brian called up the stairs.

I kissed Ben and told him to stay in bed for just a couple more minutes.

Brian stood in front of the presents we'd arranged so carefully the night before, frowning at the tree and the floor. I followed his gaze to the foil wrappers all over the rug. He picked up a stocking. White batting poked out from a two-inch hole. "They ate everything." He shook his head, not believing what he saw.

~

December melted into a frozen January. The humane methods of eradication couldn't keep up with them. Brian did such a great job of sealing the cracks in our house, the rats had no way out. He set traps and kept catching them, but they reproduced as though they were trying to take over the world, harassing me with their fertility. They chewed the bottom of our basement door, leaving teeth marks and wood shavings in their paths. They chewed the plastic components of my breast pump, set out to dry on the kitchen counter. When I discovered it, I ran upstairs and threw a plastic horn at the wall next to our bed, waking Brian.

"This is how I feed our baby!" I woke up the boys, who screamed in turn.

The rats colonized our home like little cancers. They also gave me new things to research on the internet when I was unable to sleep. I read about how one rat can turn into 1,250 rats in a single year and, in three years, produce half a billion descendants. Unlike squirrels, which breed only twice a year, rats mate constantly, with females capable of becoming pregnant within forty-eight hours of giving birth. I pictured these incestuous rats birthing, nursing, mating, and gestating, without end.

With no food for them to eat, they turned to the blocks of poison Brian placed behind our stove and refrigerator and in dark corners of the basement. They had become our common enemy, the metaphor on which to lay all our despair. We sometimes went days or even a week thinking they were gone, only to wake up and find a chewed box of cereal on the counter. I heard them behind our cupboards and hoped they were phantoms, the way I still sometimes felt a baby moving inside me. Their existence frayed the edges of my nerves and sanity.

"If nothing else, we'll set the house on fire and leave," Brian said.

I laughed, because at least now we had an escape hatch.

One snowy night, I came home from work after picking Andy up from his babysitter's house. Brian was at Cleveland State, and I had plans to take the boys over to my friend's house for dinner. Ben's day care was close to my friend's, so I stopped home to let Gus out and play with him for a few minutes. It was the hardest time of Cleveland's endless winter: dark in the morning when we left and dark again by the time we came home, a test of endurance.

After kicking the snow off my boots, I walked up the stairs and into the kitchen, where I saw a rat the size of a guinea pig staggering drunkenly across the kitchen floor. I hid Andy's car seat in the living room and called Brian, who I knew was in class. When he didn't answer, as I knew he wouldn't, I sent him a text that said, 911. Call me.

Seconds later, he was on the phone. "Are the boys okay?"

I was barely able to talk. Yes, the boys were okay. Yes, the puppy was okay. But this rat. It was at least the size of a cat; its tail was the same length as its body. Why was it moving so slowly toward Gus's water bowl?

"Tiff. The rat is dying. It must have eaten the poison."

"Why is it so big?" I could not catch my breath.

"It's probably a pregnant one."

I didn't answer. My brain was processing in slow motion, and my feet were cemented to the floor. I heard Gus whining from his crate in the dining room.

"Tiffany," Brian said, the very edge of his patience hanging on to my name. "There's a cardboard box in the basement, from the fire logs. Put the box on top of it, and then put the logs on top of the box. I'll take care of it when I'm home."

I could do that. With my dog contained in one room and my baby contained in the other, I confronted this creature, paradoxically dying and brimming with life, and left the worst of it for Brian.

SPRING 2013

The Op-Ed

There was no way of knowing as I set the box over the dying rat, but thankfully, she was the last one. Winter gave way to spring. Somewhere during this changing season, Lynch syndrome began to feel less like riding the train and more like living next to the tracks. It was still loud, but not omnipresent.

I read that more than one in every three hundred people could have Lynch syndrome, but most didn't know they were carriers. I looked for books about Lynch and found nothing but a few scattered Facebook groups with minimal traffic. I certainly wasn't going to insert myself into the support circles for patients who were actually battling cancer. Lynch was a matter of statistics, prevention, and early detection. I didn't feel like I had the right to seek support from people who had it so much worse than I did. It was lonely having a mutation I'd never heard of and, it seemed, hardly anyone else had either.

Wanting to process the feelings and experiences I was having, I started journaling, then created a blog called *Mutated, Not Broken*. But I didn't want anyone to know it was me. I didn't use my name, post any photos, or tell anyone I knew I was writing it. As far as I could see, I had one or two readers, and after a few months I stopped posting altogether. I didn't want the people I knew in real life to associate me with this mutation. The thought of sharing these deeply personal posts with people I saw every day was unbearable. Sharing my words felt like standing there naked, a nightmare I woke from with relief.

As I floated in this liminal state, clinging to my clean bill of health, Angelina Jolie published an op-ed in *The New York Times* about her decision to have a double mastectomy after learning she had a faulty BRCA 1 gene. The two breast cancer genes, BRCA 1 and BRCA 2, are like genetic cousins to Lynch syndrome, also responsible for cell repair but largely related to the breasts and ovaries rather than the colon and uterus.

Angelina Jolie wrote about her own mother's long battle with cancer, how she only got to meet one of her grandchildren, and how the others will never have the chance to experience her love themselves. She referenced the same feelings I had about protecting her children from that kind of early loss.

I wept reading this article. Everything about our lives seemed different, yet I saw my feelings reflected back to me in her story. Her details were distinct from mine, in that a mastectomy wasn't part of the Lynch syndrome protocols, but her calculus was the same. She made the decision to take seemingly drastic steps to ensure that her children knew she would do whatever it took to be with them for as long as possible. Over the next week or so, I read the backlash to this op-ed: She was attention-seeking, her type of family cancer was rare and she would push other women to undergo mastectomies who didn't truly need them, she went back to work too soon. I wanted to shake these people who hadn't faced her odds.

There was support too, of course. People admired her bravery, not just for undergoing surgery but for sharing her story. I hadn't felt brave. I felt broken. When I had told others, it was only those I trusted with the most vulnerable part of myself. It wasn't a secret, exactly, but the information felt precious. Reading that someone else, someone who seemed to exist in a different universe than I did, also dealt with a similar genetic mutation made the weight of my own burden feel a little lighter.

SPRING 2013

The Race

Brittany and I jogged down Madison Avenue, the April snowflakes swirling around us, the fluffy lake-effect flurries that movies love to capture. As we jogged past the bakeries and coffee shops, I caught my reflection in the glass. I looked like a normal person, having a regular conversation, taking a run.

I wasn't ready to open the windows yet and announce, "Hello, world! I'm alive!"

But the world had started to come back to life around me. In May I committed to running a 10k with Brittany and my dad's wife, Debbi. Debbi had been a runner her entire life, and I knew it made my dad happy for us to all run together.

"Once we hit Lincoln, you know it's three full miles, right?" Brittany pointed ahead three blocks.

"Wanna race?"

We sprinted the last three blocks, slowing down just enough to check for cars at each street crossing. I stretched my arms out at the end, and when we crossed Lincoln Avenue, elation filled me like I had finished a real race. Snowflakes floated around like candy from a piñata in the sky. I'd never run three miles without stopping, and my cheeks curved into a smile so broad my face felt tired when I relaxed them. I put my hands on my hips and tried to catch my breath.

"Now we just have to double this distance!" Brittany laughed.

I hugged her with such vigor that I caught her off balance. "We totally got it. Is this a runner's high?" I'd never felt it before. Jogging was usually a meditative chore, but I felt joyful. My legs were strong and my lungs were too; neither burned when I used them anymore.

~

Six weeks later, Brian pushed Ben's stroller through the crowds, and they cheered for us at several different spots throughout the 10k. My dad and Brittany's boyfriend, Ryan, were with them. Debbi ran more slowly than she was used to, keeping pace with Brittany and me. But I was ready, having jogged the exact distance of ten kilometers throughout Lakewood a week earlier. I stuck my tongue out at them every time I saw their arms waving in the crowd, happy for my cheering section. When we crossed the finish line, the applause from the entire crowd was so loud, with hundreds of people all cheering on their own loved ones, everyone whooping for everyone, encouraging the racers to finish strong. When I crossed under an archway of balloons, I felt the same joy I'd had when I sprinted to Lincoln in the snow. Pride surged through me, and the euphoria of finishing this race coursed through my veins. Love, even self-love, was first an action and then a feeling. One step at a time.

SPRING 2016

Unlucky

I was in a waiting room yet again. This time, my dad stood next to the window with his lips pressed into a straight line. I followed his gaze outside to a fountain pumping water into a limp arch within an empty grass lawn. Danny's wife, Jen, sat with her legs crossed as tightly as two twisted pipe cleaners while she stared just past the television screen. An unopened book rested in my lap. I felt silly thinking I could distract myself while my brother was in surgery.

A month earlier, Danny called to say he had testicular cancer. There was nothing pitiful in his voice. Just the plain, unpolished statement of an awful fact. I was alone in Andy's lime-green bedroom, attempting to restore order to his toys. Upon hearing the news, I pulled out the elf-size chair at his crayon-covered table and lowered myself into it. The room spun around me.

"Is it Lynch?" I asked. Every muscle in my body went soft.

"My urologist says no." I wanted to reach through the phone, to touch my brother and make sure he was okay. "He says it's just bad luck. Apparently, it's a young man's cancer."

Danny was thirty-two now, a full-blown adult with a house and two boxers and a wife. He brought pans of bacon and sausage to holiday brunches and had recently left his job as a bank manager because he felt uncomfortable training his tellers out of jobs by encouraging customers to switch to the mobile app. As he somehow always had, he landed on his feet and now helped places like universities and stadiums outfit their commercial kitchens.

"Have you told Dad?" I squeezed my eyes shut.

"Yeah, right before you."

I replayed this conversation in my head while the minutes ticked away in the waiting room. It was weird what you could learn to live with, given enough time. It was going on five years since we'd heard what Lynch syndrome was. While Danny's Crohn's disease would never go away, we got our colonoscopies and mostly went about our lives. But having cancer, any cancer, even a nonrelated, so-called easily treated cancer like this one, proved that we were never safe.

Not that we ever had been. In the weeks after learning this news, I kept thinking about the time Danny wrapped our dad's minivan around a telephone pole after a night of drinking when he was twenty-two. A week later, my dad took him to the impound lot to show him how much worse it could have been. It was a few months before my wedding, and I'd spent every night for weeks crying in the dark, imagining the alternate scenarios that could have left my brother or someone else dead.

I knew there was no one to blame but Danny for driving drunk, but I also knew he was struggling with the same inner demons I faced. It seemed like every time we hung out back then, we talked about our mom, as if the alcohol in our early twenties had loosened our thoughts and memories after having been sealed for more than a decade.

But here we were. Older and wiser. Watching my dad pace the length of the waiting room broke my heart. There was never any peace in parenting. I walked outside with Jen, all the way to the edge of the hospital campus to where smoking was allowed.

"I'm so sorry about this," she said, drawing her cigarette to her lips. "I keep trying to quit, but now's not the time." Jen seemed smaller than I ever remembered her being, and her Southern drawl got stronger when she was upset. She kept Danny on his toes and loved my boys so much. I didn't judge her for smoking, though I didn't want her to end up with cancer too.

"I quit, you know, before the last miscarriage," she said.

"I know." I didn't know it, but I believed her. That seemed so long ago, but it was really just a matter of months.

When Jen finished, we went back upstairs. She gripped the buzzer in her hands that would tell us Danny was moving into recovery. When it lit up like a Christmas ornament, she asked my dad and me to come back with her.

The surgeon met us in a lounge, separated from the rest of the waiting room. He still wore a paper cover over his head. There were chairs in the lounge, but nobody sat down.

"Today, Danny is cancer-free," he said.

Jen nodded her head rapidly, making her hair bounce. My dad nodded once, likely reliving all the trauma he had experienced with my mom.

The surgeon continued. "His tumor will be tested to ensure he stays that way. The results will let us know how rough the year ahead might be for him."

Danny's tumor would be sequenced to tell his medical team whether he required chemotherapy, radiation, ongoing monitoring, or some combination thereof. I didn't comprehend until that day that cancer isn't just one disease, nor is cancer of a certain organ one disease. Cancer is a collection of thousands of different diseases, each operating in its own way to edge out a body's healthy cells. I could hardly believe the enemy also held the intelligence to keep itself at bay.

JULY 2016

Sweet Adeline

The pendulum between acute grief and the purest joy never stops swinging. Danny wouldn't need treatment beyond ongoing monitoring.

At the same time Jen had her second miscarriage, Brittany found out she was pregnant. After getting married a few years earlier, she and Ryan had declared themselves child-free. I couldn't help but laugh, teasing her for still not having figured it all out by the time she was twenty-eight. But that was something about my sister—how even though I'd known her for her entire life, she never stopped surprising me. I despised myself for thinking Brittany was the lucky one once again, but I did. At the same time, I was maniacally happy for her to have a baby, for my boys to have a cousin, to share the experience of motherhood with my sister.

A week before her due date, Brian, the boys, and I were staying at a lake cottage an hour west of home, far enough to feel like a vacation and close enough to avoid the stress of traveling. It belonged to one of my friend's parents and was a place we'd visited throughout high school and college. Over the years, it had transformed from a place where we smoked pot in high school, to skinny-dipping in college, to the site of my bachelorette party, and now, to a place where I blew up rafts for my boys to paddle around on.

We'd arrived with bags of groceries to unpack and turned on the water valves. Sand peppered the grass outside, and the beach started less than fifty yards from the porch. A break wall I must have walked a hundred times stretched out at the end of the beach. To my delight, my entire family loved this place as much as I did. The boys pretended it belonged to us, even though we stayed only once a summer. I felt like the best version of myself here, like I was giving my children magical memories.

Brian was still at the beach and I was getting afternoon snacks ready when Brittany called me. "I'm at the hospital," she said. "I think the baby's coming."

I panicked. My labor with Ben was sixteen hours. Brittany had arrived at the hospital a couple of hours after us and spent the day pressing her palms into my back when I had contractions and holding a straw to my lips so I could drink ice water between pushes. I had every intention of being with her for her labor. It suddenly felt ridiculous that I thought we could sneak away so close to her due date, even for a couple of days.

"You need to be there for her," Brian said as we packed everything back up.

"We just got here!" Ben complained from the back seat. "What if we never get to come back?"

Andy looked out the window at all the signs we'd just passed earlier in the day. It was like reading a picture book backward. I felt bad for ending our getaway early and equally bad that I wasn't with my sister already.

I found Brittany with Ryan, walking the hallways in the labor and delivery unit. Her strong, muscled legs poked out from the bottom of a hospital gown. For the next several hours, we paced the halls, and then, without warning, Brittany's contractions ended. There had been no significant progression in her labor. Around midnight, the staff told her to head back home. I let myself into the house, tired and frustrated. I knew my kids would be disappointed I'd made us leave for nothing, but there was no way I wasn't going to be there for my sister.

The next morning, Ben said, "I can't believe Aunt Bee ruined our vacation and didn't even have a baby." I hated to admit I agreed with him, but I did.

"It wasn't a real vacation anyway," I said. Even though it was, for us. We went to the beach closer to home that day, and afterward I went for a walk with Brittany.

Brittany lived in my grandma's old house, less than a mile from us. For the next week, we met every day and walked through the surrounding neighborhoods. Thousands and thousands of steps. After a fruitless week, she asked if I wanted to walk the hills in the Metroparks, so we drove into the nature preserve and went up and down the edge of a steep half-mile hogback connecting the houses at the top to the valley below.

Sweat beads dotted the top of Brittany's lip. We trekked the hill several times. "I'm sorry I'm so slow," she said, laughing, as two cyclists walked their bikes past us up the hill. I loved spending these days with her as she inched ever closer to giving birth. I loved having been through this before, of having at least a little bit of wisdom to share with her, of remembering how much I felt my mother's absence at that time. I knew I was just her sister, but it made me happy to be there for her however I could.

Four days after her due date, Brittany had an appointment. She called me afterward. "The baby stopped growing." Her voice sounded like she'd either been crying or was about to. "I guess I'm getting induced today."

In the end, it was Pitocin and not the miles and miles of walking that led to my niece's birth. Like me, my sister had back labor. Ryan and I took turns shoving our hands into her lower back as hard as possible during her contractions, the same as she had for me with Ben and Andy. She amazed me, again, with her strength and stamina.

Watching my sister meet her daughter, Adeline Julia, filled me with a new kind of love. It was like the universe was balancing itself out. As Brittany cradled her baby against her chest, I saw us as girls, so young, huddled together in her bedroom after the funeral. I wished I could go back and tell them it wouldn't be easy, but they would be okay. I would promise them there was so much more love in their futures, that they were more radiant than they would ever give themselves credit for and reassure them that this horrible loss wouldn't be for nothing. I held those ghost girls in my heart, letting my love for both be a light, mothering them from the depths of my being. As my memories and this beautiful new life wove together, it created a tapestry, connecting my sister to our mom, to me, and to mothers everywhere.

FEBRUARY 2017

Beach Glass

Every year, my father-in-law, Frank, and my brother-in-law, Sam, came over for the Super Bowl. This year, the New England Patriots were losing to the Atlanta Falcons. I enjoyed making food for guests, and Frank was my favorite person to cook for. He was single, appreciated home cooking, complimented openly, and was happy to take home leftovers. This was our symbiotic relationship: one who loved to cook and one who was the perfect guest. He always arrived with flowers, a kindness he passed on to Brian.

I had made two kinds of sliders this year—hamburgers and fried chicken—both topped with pickles. Brian sent his dad a picture of the spread laid out on the bar in our newly refinished, rat-free basement, showing we were ready for him.

Sam arrived shortly before the game started. We kept waiting for Frank. During the halftime show, Ben and Andy danced to Lady Gaga when there was pounding on our side door.

"Dude, if that's Dad and he's been drinking, I'm gonna kill him," Brian said to Sam as he went up the stairs, taking two at a time.

The window to the side door looked straight down the stairs to the basement. It was immediately clear that Frank was not the one knocking. It was the police. Sam followed Brian out to the driveway and closed the door behind them. A few minutes later, Brian stood on the landing and locked the door, his face pale, and for a moment my brain flicked through possible scenarios, like Brian had been served a paternity suit, or Sam was getting arrested.

"Tiff, can you come here?" Brian called down to the basement.

Sam had taken the stairs from the landing up into our living room. My mind flashed, and I thought there must have been a car accident.

"My dad died?" Brian asked me and told me at the same time.

Frank had been found earlier that day lying in his recliner. When he didn't show up for work, the shop owner called for a wellness check. His wallet and keys were on the counter, with money and credit cards in them. There were no signs of foul play or distress.

"I just talked to him yesterday." Brian tried to make sense of this news.

Ben and Andy were seven and four years old. They held each other at the bottom of the stairs, both of their bodies shaking as tears drenched their cheeks.

"I need to call my mom," Brian said as he followed Sam, who was on the phone with Suzie already.

I knelt on the floor next to my boys and confirmed for them that, yes, their Grandpa Frank had died.

"This means now I only have one grandpa, and I already only had one grandma," Ben cried into my shoulder. "It's not fair."

The basement filled with a shock that melted into sadness later in the night, week, and months that followed. I pictured the police, two cities over, banging on the door at Sam's empty house too, grateful he was with us and not alone.

Hours later, after Brian called his aunts and uncles and we all tried to make sense of this news, we saw Tom Brady holding the Lombardi Trophy on the television.

"When did they come back and win?" Brian asked. "The old man would have loved this." I couldn't believe how much could change in an hour, or a day. I worried about how Brian would be in the coming days as the shock wore off.

The next day, Brian and I went for a walk in the Metroparks. We took the same trail we had walked over a decade earlier when we'd met the gray puppy at the shelter. Snowflakes swirled in the air. While we were out, the coroner called Brian to tell him that Frank had a heart attack in his sleep. His face and limbs were peaceful and soft. He was not in pain or afraid. Frank sat down to watch television, closed his eyes—maybe envisioning he would see his kids and grandkids the next day—and never woke up. He was sixty-two.

Brian talked about his dad, repeating stories I'd heard dozens of times. "I just talked to him," he kept saying, trying to wrap his head around how he'd gone from alive to dead so fast. Sam called, and they disagreed about whether to have his casket open or closed.

"I can't believe I have to make these decisions," he said.

"Do you want me to call the funeral home?" I offered, desperate for any way I could be helpful to him.

Brian shook his head. "I need to do this," he said.

Brian and Sam planned their dad's funeral together. When Brian asked the funeral director for a photo of his dad's eagle tattoo, wanting to get the same one, the image arrived in his text messages. It was the first time he'd seen any part of his dad's body since receiving the news, and he broke down in tears. In that moment, I realized how inadequate my own experience was when it came to comforting grown-up loss.

Over the following months, I learned how private grief is, what it means to feel helpless as someone you love tries to reconcile their past with the new present. My own stories—of illness, youth, fear, hospital beds, witnessing life limp away from the body—none of them applied here. Brian had lost his dad, and one of my only silver linings, the one saying that losing my mom had given me wisdom and my experience made me helpful to others, was suddenly irrelevant.

The grief I have lived with for most of my life is a piece of glass found on the seashore. It's been smoothed over time and can be held and rubbed absentmindedly, put in a pocket for later. I have learned how to live with this softened piece of beach glass, and despite everything, I can see beauty in it. Brian's grief was newer, his glass was sharper, it was too heavy to carry at first. Without warning and without drama, Frank had exited our lives. There was nothing I could do to make the edges of Brian's glass less sharp or help smooth them more quickly.

Brian moved his dad's belongings into our attic, poring through every scrap and file, trying to piece together the last years of his life. They'd never been as close as he was to his mom, but once or twice a year, they had the kind of interaction that sustained him. Since his father's death, Brian's never once missed the chance to provide a lesson for our sons, no matter how young they were, whether it was about putting in the effort at school or on the athletic field. In his own way, he's become like me, doing everything he can to ensure he fills the boys up, to be the dad he still wishes he had.

2017

Previvorship

The cancer center was white, its walls adorned with pieces from one of the most extensive contemporary art collections in the country, especially for a medical institution. In the waiting area, round tables held one-thousand-piece puzzles. My appointment had been bumped back twice, with my doctor needing to prioritize surgeries for patients facing immediate realities, not just probabilities like mine. These annual appointments were part of the Plan, and they put me on edge, making me question every twinge. As I checked in, I saw a woman in a headscarf leaving with her two young daughters, dissolving the self-pity that had been my companion for the past week. The teeter-totter in my heart started tilting back toward gratitude.

I sat on the exam bed across from a mirror, wrapped in a white sheet. Dr. McGinnis had been poached by one hospital system from another, and I followed him. His new space was in a gleaming, pristine ten-story vault for cancer care. I felt vain staring at myself in the mirror, imagining I had a wreath of baby's breath flowers in my hair, walking across an ivy-filled garden. There wasn't much else to do, so I posed this way and that, trying to determine if at thirty-five I was aging well, if anyone would consider me beautiful. There was a knock, and the nurse came back in. She frowned when she saw me.

"They didn't put a robe out for you?" She shuffled through the cupboard and gave me two teal robes, one to put on backward.

My English garden fantasy ended, and I was a sick person again, a shapeless heap, before the doctor came in. In cancer care and genetic terminology, I am called a "previvor," meaning a person who carries a genetic predisposition for cancer but has not had the disease. The "yet" is silent. Being a Lynch syndrome carrier, I have become an expert at navigating the airport terminal–like confusion of a major health-care institution. In fact, I am part of both a "registry" and an "institute" at the hospital, though I'm uncertain whether these are physical or virtual things. I have a coordinator who emails me periodically to ask if such and such date for my colonoscopy will work and to remind me that this year I have both an upper and lower endoscopy scheduled. Five years after my hysterectomy, breast cancer was officially added to the list of Lynch cancers. I had my first mammogram the week before this appointment, which led to my tearful second mammogram and an ultrasound as the team of doctors who oversaw my care determined my "dense breast tissue" was only part of my personal baseline and nothing worthy of a biopsy.

As a currently healthy person, I had an annual colonoscopy and a triannual upper endoscopy in which my stomach and smaller intestines were viewed by miniature cameras equipped with dollhouse-scale operating tools to remove polyps or other abnormal growths. I had the regular annual breast exams that were now augmented by mammograms and yearly skin checks to look for signs of melanoma, and my urine was tested to see if there were any red flags from my kidneys. For several years, I had taken hormonal birth control to keep my ovaries quiet. The daily reminder I was never going to have more children coupled with the irony of the hormones making me barely interested in sex would have seemed funny to me if it wasn't also true.

When I told this to Dr. McGinnis, he said, "Men have no problem telling their doctors they won't do something. Stop taking it. It's providing a small amount of protection for too high of a cost. Most ovarian cancers start in the tubes anyway, and we took those out."

I blinked away my tears, caught between embarrassment and relief. I still wanted to bargain with fate, to feel that as long as I was doing my part, cancer would remain at bay. But the reality was that a lot of my plan was about finding cancer early, not stopping it altogether.

It seemed like I was always waiting for that news, bracing myself to hear that this year was the year it had all caught up with me. It didn't help that after Frank's death, Brian and I had been meeting with a financial planner, trying to figure out how to be responsible adults. He told us that as far as life insurance went, we were underinsured. As a result, we'd both received new exams and filled out paperwork asking about our family histories and current health statuses. I received a letter in the mail informing me that my application had been denied, which I crumpled up and stuffed into the bottom of our garbage bin. According to the underwriters, my life was too risky for even a ridiculously expensive option.

I wanted Dr. McGinnis's reassurance to drip into my veins on a steady flow all day, every day. Because even though I was functional enough in my daily life, I thought about dying all the time. I saw it so clearly it scared me. I didn't only picture myself dying, transforming into the image of my mother. I imagined Brian getting in an accident or having a heart attack in his sleep and me not realizing it fast enough to call 911. I envisioned my kids pummeled by a car or falling from the monkey bars and landing on their chests, stopping their hearts. Many times, I imagined myself on the phone, needing to share this horrible news with Brian.

When I had decided to seek genetic testing, we didn't talk about the ongoing emotional toll this information might have on us. We didn't know that one day, driving home from work, Brian would pull over from dizziness, afraid he was having a stroke. How this would start to happen more frequently, and Brian would use the techniques he gave his students to talk himself through these panic attacks. There was no way of knowing that the knowledge of my faulty MSH6 gene would become a phantom third party to our relationship, lurking in our minds and memories, ready to pounce when we least expected it.

~

Over the years I stopped meeting regularly with Lou, seeing him instead when I felt the wire around my brain tightening. One of these times was after my niece was born. My boys had started asking if our family would have another baby, and I began to question whether I'd rushed my decision to have a hysterectomy.

"After they removed it, they told me that my uterus was pink and healthy, and I know that's supposed to be a good thing," I said, sitting across from Lou, stoic as ever in his sweater-vest and with his yellow notepad on the table. "But all I can picture is my healthy uterus in a biohazard bag, rotting in a landfill. Is that where it went?"

"Do you want me to answer that?"

"I think you just did." This answer upset me, and I wished I hadn't asked. "I'm supposed to be happy with two kids, and I am. And that's probably how many we would have had anyway, but now it's like that possible third baby exists out there in the universe, and I worry we made the choice for me to have surgery too fast."

"From my perspective, you made a difficult decision based on the information you had to work with. You were pretty clear in your decision while you were making it." He folded his hands together.

"But now the option is gone. And I feel bad for not being more grateful. I should feel grateful for Ben and Andy, and they should be enough."

"Practicing gratitude helps, you're right."

"But sometimes I'm sick of being grateful. I'm sick of going in circles about things that have already happened. I'm sick of thinking that I've broken everything."

"Just because you have a thought doesn't mean that it's true."

"I hate when you say therapy things to me."

Lou didn't answer me. By now, I knew his silence was an encouragement to keep talking.

"I hate how I obsess about what this does to Brian. I just wanted to show him that once in a while, he lands on the good side of a coin."

"That's a lot of pressure to put on yourself. What does he say about this?"

"He says all the right things, until he can't help himself. Then he says the worst things. He says he expects bad things will happen to him, that he'll end up like my dad or his dad, bitter and angry, and stuck with our kids, who will probably die young, and he'll end up totally alone."

"Do you think Brian would benefit from talking with me, or someone else?"

"He would, but I don't think he will." Brian ran group meetings every day and managed a caseload of students with emotional and behavioral challenges. Between me and losing his dad, he'd become the proverbial plumber with leaking pipes. He always said he knew exactly what a therapist would say to him, that he said all the same things to his students, and he just needed to work through it on his own.

Meanwhile, I had a more primal need to feel normal. Normal medically, normal behaviorally—I wanted to know that other people had the same demented thoughts that I had.

I used to ask Lou, "Is this how other people feel?" His inevitable response was some version of, "It doesn't matter how other people feel. It matters how you feel." This line of reasoning was the one branch of my tree that didn't get watered during my counseling sessions. At times like this, when I was a future zombie in the human world, I needed reassurance that my fears and how I was responding to them were normal human behavior, but that confirmation had to come from inside me and wasn't something Lou could offer.

At the same time, I was becoming a mother to older children who were trying to piece together the world as they knew it too. While resting with Ben before bed one night, he asked, "Are you not telling us there's a baby growing inside of you because you want us to be surprised when it's born?"

"No, buddy, I'm positive that there isn't a baby growing inside of me."

"How can you be sure that you're done having babies? You don't get to decide. God decides!"

There was such an innocence to these inquiries I couldn't bear to say, "Well, actually, the organ required for growing babies was cut out of my body seven years ago." Instead, I laughed and told him I was certain our family was complete.

"But how do you know?"

"Because Dad and I love you and your brother so much, and you're enough."

"Well, I wish we would have a new baby." My stomach fluttered as if on cue, activating the space where my uterus used to be. "Do you remember how cute and tiny Andy was?"

"You were that cute and tiny too!"

"But not as cute as Andy and Ada."

I rose from the bed and pulled out the photos I kept meaning to turn into an album, to show Ben how perfect he was. He said, "Yeah, I *was* really cute."

We had various versions of this conversation for several months. On my best days, this was funny and sweet to me. On my more sensitive days, these words were glaring reminders of a decision I'd made when my fear was at its highest. With several years of good health between my positive test and now, I wished I'd given myself more time to weigh my options. My baby years were over, while for several of my friends and colleagues, they were just beginning.

Previvorship evoked a mental battle to be grateful I wasn't sick, while being hyperaware of the alternate future my team of doctors and I plotted to avoid. I had so many tests, each one stoking my anxiety in the days and weeks leading up to them. Every time a test result came back negative or I was declared clear for another year, I was relieved. But it was also exhausting to be under constant surveillance. I felt like

I was perpetually at odds with my body, never trusting it, even though it kept doing exactly what it was supposed to.

One day I was cleaning Andy's room, and out of nowhere, everything looked like a broken mirror. I sat on his rug and tried to focus. After several minutes, convinced I had a brain tumor, Brian drove me to the emergency room. Just as suddenly, my vision returned, and the medical team almost laughed at my textbook-perfect description of an ocular migraine. They sent me home and told me to go to sleep, warning that a headache would be following close behind. I would go days or weeks without thinking about this at all before being struck with the worry I had forgotten to schedule some appointment, or what was that pain in my side?

Another day right after lunch, I left my office, walked to the hospital down the street, and waited for an X-ray of my back. I'd had pain that would not go away, despite stretching and visits to the chiropractor. I pictured myself filling up with tumors a colonoscopy would miss. Three hundred dollars later, the doctor confirmed I had no tumors, only an almost negligible amount of arthritis in a very small portion of my back. The doctor told me to practice good posture and perform core-strengthening exercises. It was both a relief and total humiliation to see myself turning into such a hypochondriac.

That night, after the boys smeared the cheese from their quesadillas on the dining room table and I was wiping sour cream from the back of a chair, I told Brian about walking to the emergency room. "So, I have good news," I said, and recounted the visit.

Brian stood up from the table and brought his hand to his chin, stroking his short beard like it was a blanket. "You didn't even tell me anything was bothering you. Don't you realize I wait around, every year, for the results of your colonoscopies? Do you remember I slept at the hospital after your surgery? I never want to hear about you doing something like this, alone, ever again. Don't fucking lie to me, Tiffany."

I met his dark, angry eyes and felt my skin flush. "But I wasn't lying to you."

"How do I know what you do all day long now? How am I supposed to trust you?"

"I just did it today. And here I am, telling you. Today." I held my arms out wide, so certain of my stance.

"No." He folded his arms over his chest. "Telling the truth would be telling me before you went that you were on your way. Or telling me that you were worried something was wrong before today."

I pressed my palms into my stinging eyes. "You're right," I said, admitting defeat.

In trying to shield him from my fears, I had shut him out of my thoughts and caused him pain in the process. Early on in my mom's illness, I'd learned that there was no room for my fears. "I can't understand you when you're crying, Tiffany," my dad would say. I became good at not crying by not talking about things that would make me cry. There was too much happening physically for any of us to deal with imaginary things like thoughts. My habit became to keep them all to myself.

When Brian and I started dating, he accused me of being shady, implying I had secrets. But I didn't have secrets, I had *feelings*. I had feelings I'd had no practice learning how to express. I just wasn't in the habit of retelling each day's events, assuming the details of my life weren't newsworthy. Over time, he asked me questions about my days and my life and listened intently when I answered him. It was the greatest gift in the world to talk about things I'd kept inside, things I didn't even realize were desperate to be expressed. But when I was scared, I went back inside. When something was too hard for me to face, it seemed easier to shield him as well. It took me until this argument to understand the toll my habit of facing things alone placed on him. On us.

SPRING 2018

Scar Tissue

Once again, I found myself sitting next to Danny's wife, Jen, in a waiting room—this time for his colonoscopy. A home-makeover show played on the nearby television, its closed captions lagging behind the dialogue. I stared out the window at nothing in particular. The tinted glass cast a shadow over the city, making it look like a storm was on its way.

"Danny is my whole world," Jen said nervously. "I don't know what I'd do without him. I just know this time is going to be bad news. He hasn't been taking his Crohn's medication, and I know it's not under control." She spun her wedding ring around her finger, like it was a bottle cap that wouldn't tighten. "I've been having the biggest fights of my life with him, about picking a medication and sticking with it, but he keeps saying he's fine. I feel like a terrible wife, because I needed to stop fighting with him about it, but now? That's why I asked you to come, so if there is bad news, I have someone else to hear it with me. I can't manage him on my own."

I nodded, the weight of the burden Jen and Brian both carried hitting me as I listened to Jen's confession and nervous chatter. Sitting on this side of the waiting-room door was harder than I expected. I wasn't made for waiting. I gained new empathy for Brian, who clock-watched his way through these exams every year. I thought back to my college philosophy classes and the Stoic named Seneca who said, "We suffer more in imagination than we do in reality." These waiting rooms overflowed with the possibilities of what may come. I tried to tell myself things like *That's a problem for Future Tiffany*, but it was hard to witness up close the anxiety Jen, Brian, and my dad carried.

"He's been avoiding Dr. Clark since his surgery last year." Jen turned over the black buzzer in her hands, the one that would light up when Danny was done. She noted the time on her phone.

Danny hadn't scheduled his colonoscopy earlier because, as he'd told me, he needed "a fucking break from a clinical setting." It was a hard cycle to be in, bracing himself for bad news every couple of months to ensure the testicular cancer remained at bay. I was mad at him for being late, while also understanding his need to protect his psyche.

"These have been some awful years, haven't they? He's lucky I love him so much," Jen said, faking a smile.

"We're all lucky you love him so much." I took a deep breath. "Jen, I think you're being too hard on yourself. Danny's a grown-up. I know how impossible it is to make Brian do anything he doesn't want to do." She nodded, and I nodded in return.

I have a recurring dream, usually in the weeks leading up to my own colonoscopies. In the dream, I'm in the waiting room, ready to head back into the exam room, and I realize I forgot to prepare for it. I begin to panic as I determine if I should fess up and tell the doctors my bowels are still thick with stool, in which case I would have to reschedule my appointment for several months in the future, or if I should attempt to have the colonoscopy done anyway. I'm so mad at myself. How did I forget the most important part of this process?

In real life, on multiple occasions, as I've stared at the wall waiting for the nurses to wheel me into my procedure, I've heard patients who are coming out of their appointments being told they would have to reschedule. They had either not prepped at all or had prepped half-assed (pun fully intended), not allowing the doctor to see what she was looking for. They are usually waking up from the twilight sleep when this news is delivered, their answers groggy, and I wonder if they will remember when they get home that the procedure wasn't complete.

Less than forty minutes after Danny went back, the buzzer in Jen's hands went off. It was too fast. Jen bolted upright and went toward the back. I followed her through the doorway separating the waiting room from recovery. My nightmare, in which I was told I had to come back for a repeat procedure, happened in real life to Danny this time.

Dr. Clark met us outside the curtain where Danny was in recovery. His Crohn's was so severe, with his intestines so inflamed, the procedure was not completed. He would require a round of heavy steroids before he could return in eight weeks for a follow-up. The doctor's office would be contacting him for a meeting with Dr. Kantor, the head of the digestive disease clinic, to discuss his surgical options.

Over the years I've learned that bad medical news is given as factually as good news, and this case was no different. I sat with Jen while she repeated the words to Danny as he woke up. When she needed a break, I repeated them to him, but he wasn't ready to hear this news yet.

It wasn't until I emerged from the parking garage and was driving in to work that Danny's news hit me. My entire body tightened. Not Danny, not again. I couldn't breathe. I rolled down the windows, and the cold air roared into the car, drowning out my thoughts that he was so much sicker than we knew. How could he have let this happen? I knew it wasn't fair to blame him, but I needed it all to make sense. Dr. Clark had said his Crohn's was making it impossible to screen for colon cancer.

I'd met Dr. Kantor, the surgeon, only once. He had dark hair, protruding eyebrows, and a serious face. Danny and I each met him separately years earlier, and the message was, "You won't see me again unless you need surgery."

Surgery, in my family's case, equaled cancer. But now my expectations inverted. As an outsider, I understood Crohn's to be a painful nuisance, not the real enemy. Now, though, the inflammation and scarring in Danny's intestines was bad enough on its own that surgery to remove the affected portion was necessary. Dr. Kantor said he didn't see a future for Danny in which surgery was not an option. The question was how much colon to remove and how soon. Like me with my uterus, Danny wasn't sure how long he could trust his body.

Over the next couple of weeks, he and Jen discussed the options the surgeon had presented them: attempting to control his Crohn's medically, which had been unsuccessful in the past and was potentially too far gone; removing the inflamed portion of his intestines, which could put his Crohn's in remission for a few months or a few years; or removing his entire colon and rectum and creating a stoma, which is a hole in the abdomen that allows the small intestine to empty into a plastic pouch.

In the first two options, Danny would constantly be on the lookout for signs that Crohn's had spread farther up his digestive tract, possibly all the way up to his esophagus. He would also still have annual colonoscopies. The third option, the most drastic, removed his risk of colon and rectal cancer and meant he could control when the surgery took place. He wouldn't have to worry about signing up for a partial colectomy, only to wake up to the news that the entire organ had to be removed. He could cross off his highest-risk cancer from the churning mental list of things that kept him awake at night and caused Jen to quiet her nerves with nicotine.

I was helping Ben with his homework at the dining room table when Danny called me. I held up one finger to Ben and went upstairs to my bedroom.

"How did you decide to have your hysterectomy?" Danny asked. "For Jen, option three is the only option. My brain knows that's the right thing to do, but I need some time to get my heart to that place too. I'd never take another shit," he said, laughing, "so I have that going for me."

I wanted to laugh at his joke in return, but the backs of my thighs prickled with goose bumps. Even as I understood the necessity of the full colectomy, it still inspired a visceral reaction when I pictured it.

"Well, I already had kids," I said. "My uterus became an internal ticking time bomb. I worried constantly about this part of my body turning into Mr. Hyde, broken cell after broken cell, multiplying on themselves, infecting the rest of my organs."

"Yeah, I'm the same way right now. Plus, you know, it's hard with Jen. She says it's up to me, but I can't keep doing this to her, over and over."

For Danny and me and other people who have their genetic mutations memorized, we want to remain healthy for ourselves, and we need to respect the fear and anxiety our cancer risks instill in the people we love, particularly our spouses, who have chosen to love and build futures with us. So long as we are the storm pulling the roof off the house, we need to believe we can also hammer it back into place.

"Surgery just seems drastic to people who don't have to make the choice," I said. "But the longer you live with the possibility, the less scary it becomes."

"I guess I'd rather have one major surgery and be done with it than keep worrying about needing to have another one. Nickel-and-diming away my colon."

"I also felt a responsibility to protect the innocence of the boys," I said. "I never want to traumatize them if I can help it. I don't want them to grow up in a house that smells like a hospital or not know me as teenagers and adults. I can't leave them with a dad suffocating in his own grief."

"Jen left her entire family to live in a state with six months of winter," Danny said, "for me. I'm having the surgery. The whole thing. I'm not putting her through any more of this."

It wasn't until we talked that I realized how strongly I felt about all these medical decisions. They were such private choices, but their impact went beyond just the one being operated on. They'd given me the ability to keep fighting for my family as much as for myself. It was weird to keep understanding myself better and better the more I kept facing the things I was most afraid of.

SUMMER 2020

Eleven

The summer Ben was eleven, we took a family trip to the Canaan Valley in West Virginia. We were four months into the pandemic and desperate to escape the confines of our house. We sought a place far away from the COVID hot spots where we could be outside and look at a different landscape than the one we felt trapped inside at home.

Before this trip, I'd thought of West Virginia as a place to drive through quickly on our way to the ocean. But as we approached, the mountains spread out around us, vast as an ocean themselves. Our cabin was in an off-season ski town called Davis. We were less than five hours from home, but these mountains felt as foreign to me as another country. Our cell phones barely worked, and all the directions we found referenced natural features or landmarks we couldn't identify.

On our second day, I'd made reservations for us to go horseback riding. It's only in retrospect that I can see the parallels in getting to a state with mountains and putting my eleven-year-old on a horse. Back then, I'd been desperate to escape, but now I wanted to make memories with my boys. Their lives had been so different from mine, so blissfully uneventful, until the pandemic hit, of course. Along with the uncertainty we all faced globally, I found myself grappling with the knowledge that I'd soon have a child older than my mom ever had the chance to see me become. I felt, deep inside, how strange it would be to navigate motherhood without a road map.

Ben wore glasses and had a great sense of humor. We'd invested in braces earlier in the summer, and he started smiling with his teeth showing for the first time in ages. He was still shorter than I was. By the next summer, I guessed he'd surpass me. Most of all, I soaked in every bit of him that was still a child.

While we waited in the shop connected to the farm for our horses to be ready, Andy and Ben nervously touched the T-shirts and trinkets. They argued with me about wearing helmets, and I appreciated the handwritten sign next to the register that declared ALL RIDERS UNDER 16 MUST WEAR A HELMET. After swiping our credit card, we walked back toward the barn and the boys grew quiet, noticing how large the horses were.

"You always make me do things I don't want to do," Brian muttered. I didn't ask him if he meant horseback riding specifically or West Virginia generally or leaving home altogether, but I imagined in that moment it was a little bit of each.

"At least everyone was wearing a mask," Andy's raspy voice chimed in as he shrugged his shoulders.

All saddled up, several guides took us out as part of a much larger group. With my horse's warm back between my thighs, we went up and down several trails, demystifying these hypnotic mountains by opening up their views to green valleys, open sky, and magnetic blue waves that went on forever, the mountain ranges all around us.

A visit to the mountains mirrored the strange mood of this pandemic summer. The ache, the mystery, the depth, stood in stark contrast to the lightheartedness of our usual lake or ocean vacations. The brooding West Virginia peaks seemed to embody the anxiety we'd all been teetering on the edge of. I didn't know when, or if, the boys would ever return to school, if my office would ever reopen, when we could safely see our families again. We were supposed to keep on living our lives, but tethered to computer screens in a way that made it feel like there was no privacy on either end of the nonstop Zoom calls, meetings, and classes. My kids had learned my colleagues' voices and tics, while my coworkers had seen me explaining fractions and biting my tongue when the boys fought. Our nerves stretched and pinched at home. I felt the same sense of claustrophobia driving through the mountains—as if at any moment, the road would give way around an unseen bend.

Once I was inside the mountains on horseback, however, I no longer felt trapped by them. My horse moved underneath me, strong but careful. At each turn, new vantage points emerged, the mountains revealing themselves to us in ways that would have been impossible to see from the roads.

After being nervous about mounting their horses, I saw my sons gaining confidence as the ride unfolded. Andy stopped clutching his reins and relaxed his arms. He sat up straighter. Ben stroked his horse's neck. Brian gave them both a thumbs-up when the paths allowed them to see each other. I saw pride on the boys' shoulders for doing something they were unsure of and having survived.

"That was a turning point," Brian declared when we returned to the stable, his smile broad under the wide-open sky. I didn't ask if he meant on this trip, or this summer, or in our lives. I felt it for all of them and decided to believe he did too. Ben was eleven, and I was still here.

~

That autumn, Ben started sixth grade. I felt myself reliving the fall when I was his age. I observed him even more carefully, savoring him. We rearranged his bedroom and set it up for virtual learning. I stole whiffs of the new, sweaty smell he produced. I bought him deodorant, and his hair changed from blond to light brown. As much as I wanted him to start middle school with his friends and for everything around us to be normal again, I also couldn't believe I got to have him so close to me at this precious age.

Brian and I put our worries aside and held our breath as Ben rode his bike around Lakewood, meeting his masked friends at the park at the end of their virtual school days, grasping for fragments of normality, unsure of what would be safe in the long run and what we might regret. He was growing up and gaining independence, just as he was supposed to.

He worried about what we'd have for dinner, whether there would be basketball that winter, if the kids at school would notice he'd had braces when he went back. I asked Brian if he seemed immature, and Brian laughed at the question. "He seems exactly like a sixth-grade boy," he'd answered.

I couldn't put this young boy next to my memories of myself at his age. I'd felt so old, so grown up, not at all like a child. But the faces of the girls on his Zoom screen looked so fresh and earnest, not even adolescent yet. I must have looked like them. I must have sounded like them.

As the first Saturday in October approached, I imagined my mom looking at me, my sister, and brother. I pictured her searing images of us into her memory, afraid of everything she might never see: the graduations, weddings, first loves and heartbreaks, the ordinary moments that make up the daily rhythms of a home, hoping she'd given us enough love to last a lifetime. That Saturday morning, I snuck into my boys' rooms while they were still sleeping, watching the gentle rise and fall of their chests, inhaling the salty smell of their skin after a night of sleep. I soaked in Ben's perfect youth, admiring the beautiful threshold he occupied between child and teenager.

The realization of how young I had been when I had felt so grown washed over me. Now, I was not only older than my mom had ever been, but my child was becoming older than the version of me she had known. To survive her impending death, I'd had to start imagining I could survive it before it happened. Slowly, I let the shame around my mom's death dissolve, releasing the guilt that I had somehow given up on her.

This milestone date came and went, a watershed moment existing only inside of me. If newborn Ben allowed me to forgive my mother for dying, then preteen Ben helped me to forgive myself for all the impossibly heavy feelings I carried for so many years. He showed me I'd been such a young girl, that nothing I said or did or felt had made me responsible for any of it.

PART THREE

SUMMER 2021

Rest Peacefully

Just after we all received our first COVID vaccines, my grandma was diagnosed with liver cancer. We'd already missed Thanksgiving and Christmas and an entire year of birthdays. It seemed wildly unfair that as soon as we could all safely see each other without masks again, we were losing her. I took off a day of work each week between her diagnosis and death, not sure how much time I had with her. For seven weeks, my Aunt Jenny and I went through what she kept after years of purging the scraps that remained important enough for her to hold on to.

Visiting her made me sad, of course. But it also made me feel whole, like I could be strong and steady for my grandma, as she had always been for me. I made grilled cheese sandwiches and heated cans of soup for lunch, curled onto the bed the hospice workers delivered, and I listened. I opened and snapped shut the jewelry boxes holding necklaces with matching clip-on earrings I never remembered her wearing and turned over photographs to read the cursive writing on the back indicating names and years.

Danny, Brittany, and I texted each other constantly. I cry randomly, all day long, Brittany confessed.

Same, Danny and I echoed.

I thought I was prepared for this, but I wasn't, Danny wrote.

Frank showed me childhood loss does nothing to prepare us for adult grief, I answered.

This must be what it feels like when your parents are dying, Brittany wrote.

~

"How long will it take you to get over it?" Ben asked me when I explained that my grandma would never get better. "Never get better" being the sanitized way of saying "is actively dying."

We were on our way to Andy's baseball game, well practiced in the art of running from one sporting event to the next, eating sandwiches for dinner on the sidelines.

"I'm not sure you ever get over it when someone dies. You just learn how to live with your sadness, and it stops taking your breath away, like over time it becomes more manageable somehow."

"But how long will you cry for?" He wanted a time stamp on the paralyzing form of grief. I'd been foggy all week, forgetting the date. My body showed up to work, my thoughts were anywhere but. I ordered too much takeout and ran out of toilet paper.

"I'm not sure, honestly." I knew I should capitalize on my twelve-year-old's curiosity and be living proof that death is survivable. I felt shallow instead, like any answer I provided would be fake.

"There's a kid in my grade, and his life has been horrible, just like yours. But he's okay now."

"What do you mean, 'just like' mine?"

"Well, his might even be worse than yours. Both of his parents died when he was a baby, and he had to get adopted by the parents he has now, who are really nice."

It hurt to hear Ben boil my life down like that, like I hadn't spent enough time focusing on the good things in my life or sharing what I'd learned from it. Maybe my perception of myself was more negative than

I realized. "I love my life," I said a few breaths too late, barely sounding convincing to myself. We pulled into the baseball diamond.

He unlocked his door and asked, "I can have the roast beef, right?"

I assigned oceans of value to these moments, to the glimmers that somewhere on the other side of puberty, a sensitive and kind person would burst from the chrysalis manifesting this full-body transformation.

Ben had already set up our folding chairs and was talking to his Grandma Suzie by the time I applied my sunscreen and walked over.

"You hanging in?" she asked.

I nodded, because talking and receiving love at the same time would have cracked me open like a walnut shell, and I needed to remain whole. She understood because compassion was what she did best. We shifted gears and watched Andy's team play, interrupting for snippets in which I told her I thought it would be only a few days, at most.

"You're a tough lady." I felt anything but tough, but hearing these words made the waning flame inside me brighten.

The next night, I left Ben's baseball game and waited for Brian to come home. He'd been coaching Andy's team in another city, and I didn't want to leave for my grandma's before seeing him. I told him about the play Ben made at third base and the run he drove in. We had a drink in our backyard, beneath the open sky and towering oak trees.

"It will probably be tonight," I said.

"Do you really need to go?" he asked.

"I'd do the same thing for your mom." A cloud of gnats clung together like static against the periwinkle sky. Every muscle in my body told me I needed to be with my grandma, to hold her hands as they grew thick with fluid, to sit bedside with my aunt, who had been caring for her around the clock.

"I know. I'm sorry."

I took a sip of my beer, prolonging the inevitable and afraid of being too late, suspending myself in the before and after of losing her.

~

Jenny's living room was quiet but filled with the invisible energy of emotions running at full speed. My grandma lay in the hospital bed, her arms and fingers filling with the fluids her body no longer flushed into a bag hanging by her feet. It held the same amount of dark urine as it had earlier that day, showing us her systems were shutting down.

I was sandwiched on the sofa between Danny and Brittany. Along the back wall, our grandma's eyes were closed. Her chest moved up and down with shallow, jagged breaths. Across from us, Jenny sat in the recliner that had been my grandma's until she stopped being able to sit a few days before.

Earlier in the evening, we shared our favorite stories, many of which were the compromising situations we put our grandma in over the years. "Remember the water slide?" Danny laughed so hard, he could barely talk. "She went airborne on that second drop, and I felt so bad!"

"How about when we accidentally left her standing in the rainstorm in Edinburgh?" Brittany chimed in. "We were in the taxi and drove right past someone standing in a blue poncho, saying we felt bad for them to be out in such horrible weather?" Brittany picked up our grandma's puffy, limp hand and, through her laughter, she said, "I'm so sorry we left you out there!"

None of these stories were new confessions, just the rehashing of a lifetime of memories with our matriarch, a woman we all loved without bounds. During the passing hours, our laughter melted into quiet memories, our vigil a suspension of normal time.

That morning, I had sat on the bed and wrapped my arms around her. "How are you doing, Grandma?" I made my voice as cheerful as possible.

Her words slurred a bit, but she answered, "I'm okay." She paused as confusion moved into her face like a front. "I'm not sure I know who you are, though."

"Grandma, it's Tiff. Julie's oldest daughter, your first granddaughter."

Her yellowed eyes turned glassy with tears that didn't fall. She squeezed my hand with hers. I held this hand for the next hour as she fell in and out of sleep and wiped away my own tears.

Nearly three of my mom's lifetimes could fit inside her eighty-seven years. Maybe I wouldn't have been sitting there with my grandma if my mom were alive to hold her hands. Maybe my mom would have fed her tiny bites of watermelon earlier in the day, while I was off somewhere else, being someone else. Maybe Danny, Brittany, and I wouldn't all live within a mile of each other, all of us here, together.

The room grew quiet. I remembered the night we lost Jeff, and I imagined my mom's death being similar, a terrible thing you don't want to happen but are afraid to miss. I thought it was incredibly generous for Jenny and Pat to inscribe this memory into their living room, allowing my grandma's breath to shorten at home instead of among the mechanical beeps of a hospital.

I felt a question I'd carried tightly for almost three decades rumble to life inside me. We'd watched my mom die for so long, yet I still didn't understand why she'd never said goodbye. "When did my mom know she was going to die?" I asked.

"I don't think," Jenny said, smoothing the blanket over her lap, "your mom ever accepted she was going to die." My grandma had stopped nodding along with our stories, but her chest kept rising and falling.

"You don't remember the story?" Brittany asked.

I shook my head. "What story?"

"She was sitting on her bed," Brittany said, turning her eyes away from our grandma and toward me. "She picked up the mirror on one of her powder puffs, the rose-scented one. She felt something on her stomach, and she used the mirror to look at it." This story was coming back to me, but one word at a time, like headlights piercing through a blizzard. "It was her tumor growing through her skin. She completely freaked out on Dad, who had been telling her every day that she was getting better, that her skin was healing. She told him she hated him for lying to her, that she didn't trust him anymore, and she never wanted to see him again. He had to call Grandma to come take care of Mom that night, because she refused to see him."

"She had tubes for her kidneys," Jenny said, "and was on Ativan and morphine. I asked her if she ever thought about writing to you kids, but she didn't want to do it. She only agreed to hospice two days before she died. Brittany, do you remember the blood?"

With these words, our Uncle Pat emerged from the kitchen, where he had been keeping himself busy putting away dishes and wiping the already spotless countertops. "Oh, Britt, it was so bad. Your grandma and dad took your mom to the hospital, and I came to stay with you. There was blood everywhere, and I made you stay upstairs while I tried to clean it." His black eyebrows squished together, merging into a single caterpillar. "No child should ever see that. I remember you started to come downstairs."

"Did you see it?" Jenny repeated.

Brittany clasped her hands around each of her elbows, like she was giving herself a hug. "I sometimes don't remember what I actually saw or did with my mom and what people tell me about her. I do remember this story, though."

"She was never ready to go." Jenny's nervous energy and conviction made these words come out with force I wasn't expecting. "She was really bitter about it. I remember her thirtieth birthday, and she said most of her friends took trips with their husbands and she got cancer. It was impossible for her to let go."

"I knew why you had us write her notes," I said. "But to be honest, I've always been a little mad that she never wrote us anything herself."

"I felt that way too," Britt said, her voice low.

I believed she was dying for months before it happened. To hear that on the brink of death, my mom refused to believe it herself took my breath away. As every system in our mother's body shut down, the last part of her to die was her hope.

The minutes kept passing by. We kept talking, both to each other and to our grandma, reassuring her that we were here, we loved her, and that it was okay to let go. Around two o'clock in the morning, Danny stood up and stretched. "I have to get to work in the morning," he said before hugging us all goodbye. After his departure, Brittany and I snuggled into the couch, our heads at opposite ends. Jenny leaned back in the recliner. I closed my eyes and listened to my grandma's breath. In and out. In and out. In and out. In and nothing.

Nothing but the quiet of her unreleased exhale. My sister sat straight up. "Do you hear that?"

We both rose from the couch to our grandma's bed. Brittany picked up her hand and placed two fingers on her wrist. I laid my palm on her warm, still chest.

"Anything?" I whispered.

Brittany shook her head the tiniest bit, unsure about committing to this answer.

"Is she okay? Does she need anything?" Jenny's sleepy voice asked.

"We think she's gone," one of us said.

The three of us stood around her. Jenny said a prayer. In a single, fleeting moment, she passed from living to dead—a blink of disbelief, followed by calm. Our sadness swirled with relief and the solemn honor of being there with her until the end.

~

Later that night, after the men from the funeral home took away her body and after Jenny went through all the leftover medications with the hospice nurse, after I wrote her obituary and found a beautiful photo to accompany it, and after I tried and failed to take a nap, we were all home, miraculously, without any baseball games. Instead, we watched the Indians game from our couch while exhaustion worked itself deep within my muscles. Andy's warm, wiry body wiggled into mine.

After several innings, I told him it was time for bed.

He pressed his face into my thigh and tightened up.

"Baby, what's wrong?"

"I know your grandma just died," he cried. "And I'm sad about that. I really am."

I rubbed his back, sensing he wasn't done. He sat up, his face red and wrinkled, his cheeks wet.

"But now I can't get out of my head how you're going to die too someday." He collapsed into my chest for a hug, and I pulled him close. "I never want that to happen," he said.

Andy relaxed, the weight of his fears lifting from his body as if by invisible cables, and I didn't know if I'd ever loved him more.

FALL 2021

Oophorectomy

I bought a blue tie-dye dress for my grandma's funeral. It reminded me of water and her favorite clothes. Our family stood in a circle among the gravestones while I read her eulogy. I called my grandma a lighthouse: always present, calm amid storms, a beacon of light in the darkness. I said that my grandma taught me what bravery looks like. It wasn't always swimming across a nearly freezing mile-wide river, though it did look like that once for her. It was living your life with the clear acceptance of what it was and not being destroyed by what it wasn't.

Ben had been to the cemetery once before, as a toddler, after Jeff died. Andy had never been. Both of my boys squatted down in front of my mom's grave. I think they wanted to feel something, a closeness or a warmth, that stones can't provide. We laid daisies on all the gravestones. Afterward, we had dinner at a restaurant overlooking the aquamarine Saint Clair River. Cars and bikes rode by on the other side, and like I'd been as a child, my sons were amazed that an entirely different country was just right there.

Four weeks later, I was back in Dr. McGinnis's office. I knew the artwork in the cancer center's corridors by heart, just as I knew my own rhythms of fear, anxiousness, relief, and distraction. It was September, and a few weeks earlier I'd had a clean colonoscopy, the fourth clean one in a row, which was the longest I'd ever gone without having a polyp to remove. My gastroenterologist credited the high dose of aspirin I took each day. It was the kind of good news I was afraid to trust, as though I might jinx myself just by acknowledging this at all.

As I reconsidered the paradox of being a healthy person who is treated like a sick person, a polite knock on the door snapped me back to the room. It wasn't until Dr. McGinnis asked how I was feeling about my upcoming birthday that my dread surfaced, a frozen block of ice stored deep inside beginning to thaw.

"Any breakthroughs yet?" I felt the side of my mouth quiver. I would be forty in a few months, the deadline we had given my ovaries a decade earlier hovering ever closer.

He shook his head. "I wish."

Medicine hasn't come up with a better solution to ovarian cancer risk than removal. This abstract surgery had been a box I sat inside of, shrinking around me each year. It's called an oophorectomy, its name almost as impossible to pronounce as it was for me to imagine happening to my body. These almond-shaped organs controlled so much that their smallness confounded me.

My ovaries were not just for reproduction, as my uterus had been. Although ovaries are most associated with releasing eggs, they are also adrenal glands contributing to overall health. They produce estrogen, a chemical charged with regulating bone strength, breast and vaginal health, cognitive function, and the overall aging process. They also produce testosterone, best known as a male sex hormone but which women have in small amounts as well, and that helps with libido, cardiovascular health, weight maintenance, and our musculoskeletal system.

Even though they were so small, having my ovaries removed felt much more drastic than my hysterectomy, and I worried not only about my physical recovery but my chemical one as well.

"You have some time," Dr. McGinnis said. "To get yourself used to it."

"How much time?" I didn't think I would ever be ready for this surgery in the way that someone is ready to have children or anything else irreversible. I knew turning forty was the end zone I was marching toward, and he was trying to give me a sense of control. I'd been getting ready for ten years. I leaned back on the exam table, and he prodded my abdomen.

"I'd do it within the year," he said. After a decade of these exams, I trusted him and the careful way he spoke.

Dr. McGinnis ordered an appointment with a women's health specialist. When I should have been working, I revisited the online forums I used to read, pages and pages of women sharing their new Lynch syndrome diagnoses. As I read these forums, I remembered why I pulled back in the first place. Returning to that dark, bewildering time when everything was impossible and overwhelming made me feel worse. I felt terrible for all of these perfectly normal women and understood the shifting reality they sought to make sense of, yet I also needed some distance from that fresh wound.

On my fifteenth wedding anniversary, I met the women's health specialist, Dr. Turner. She had bright red hair and wore a dress the same forest green my mom said looked good on me. "I see women in their seventies, eighties, even nineties," she told me. She spoke like she was from a big New England family and had learned how to fight for airtime. "Of course, we'll order you estrogen. You can start that the same day as your surgery. You're taking hormone replacement, right? You're so young. Why would you want to feel bad?" I envied her energy levels and assumed she practiced what she was preaching.

I thought about how I tortured myself through two drugless labors and deliveries. Now that my sons were older, I couldn't remember what I had tried to prove to myself. But there was euphoria when the births were over, with the immediate cessation of searing pain and overwhelming feelings of love and gratitude and relief. I knew surgical menopause wouldn't be like that.

We reviewed the blood work and bone-density scan she ordered. Since I hadn't had a period in over a decade, a secret part of me hoped I'd already entered menopause. My kids were older, and they aggravated me. My work aggravated me. Brian and I aggravated each other. All of this amid a global pandemic and the grief over losing my grandma. It would be a convenient gift from the universe to learn that my ovaries sucked anyway and my bad mood could be solved with an estrogen patch. Instead, she told me my ovaries functioned perfectly, my muscle tone was great, and I had some of the best bones she'd ever seen. "Granted, most of my patients aren't active thirty-nine-year-old women!"

She asked me what vitamins I took and shook her head when I said a multivitamin, sometimes. "Vitamin D, at a minimum. I'd like you on magnesium and calcium too." She rattled this all off with an efficiency that made me trust her.

I scheduled the surgery for January, three weeks after my fortieth birthday. I didn't want to admit how important this birthday was for me, what a milestone it was to leave my thirties. Brian and I didn't talk much about the surgery leading up to it. We distracted ourselves with Christmas and by driving all over northeast Ohio to watch the boys play basketball, grimacing about all the places where nobody wore masks and feeling guilty for being out in public at all. I made grand plans to have the healthiest January of my life and going into surgery as strong as I'd ever been.

In reality, I cooked more cheesy pasta than I'd ever eaten and drank more wine than I want to admit. I didn't exercise at all. I wrote bad poetry and took long baths, nourishing my soul if not my body, and giving my fears space. Something started shifting in me. I'd kept exercising over the years: Jogging turned into high-intensity interval training, which led me to start lifting weights. But I always felt I should be leaner, fitter, tighter. When I looked in the mirror, I saw my soft stomach, my sagging breasts, the wrinkles etched into my forehead like lines on paper. Instead of appreciating everything my body had done right over the years, I was still mad at it for being mutated and outside my control. It occurred to me during this time that maybe I should stop punishing my body for its flaws and try loving it instead, imperfections and all.

One night as I lay in the bathtub, savoring one of the soaks I wouldn't be able to have during recovery, I tried to figure out my feelings about the upcoming procedure. I wasn't afraid of anesthesia or of surgery going wrong. I wasn't afraid of an infection or the pain of recovery. I placed my hands on my stomach, making a heart-shaped frame around my belly button with my thumbs and forefingers. It moved up and down with each breath. I whispered "thank you" to my body or to the universe, or to both. I thought a lot about my uterus and my breasts, these parts of me that seemed so fully female. But my ovaries were what made me a woman. I was afraid that by having this medically simple surgery, I might lose the essence of who I was.

Five days before my surgery, I had a pre-op appointment with Dr. McGinnis. "I'm scared of menopause," I said, finally understanding myself. "Of mood swings and depression, of something inside me changing forever." An embarrassed laugh squeaked out of my mouth, a frustrating nervous tic. My hysterectomy was about losing my fertility, but this surgery invoked a fear of losing my personhood or personality.

"We'll take care of you," Dr. McGinnis said, making a promise I hoped he could live up to.

It freaked out Brian too. Our relationship had been defined by a willingness to talk about everything, but the months leading up to surgery were quieter, yet stormier than usual. Our tempers were short, and we both protected our feelings, even from each other. He was afraid, too, of all the same things I was. But I was more afraid of what might happen if I didn't have the surgery.

"I would never be able to look the boys in the eyes and tell them I have cancer if I haven't done what I could to prevent it," I finally said out loud one night as I changed into my pajamas. I wanted him to see me, to touch me, to remind me that he loved me.

Brian nodded, but his eyes focused on something on the wall. "I know you have to do it." White hairs peppered his dark beard, age and nerves moving across his skin like glaciers. We were both resigned, both as ready as we'd ever be.

The sunrise on the morning of my surgery was magenta and purple. I stood by my bedroom window to watch the red glow of the sun peek through the two houses across the street. By the time we left, the white

January clouds covered up the sun, and I felt like it was good luck I'd seen the first, stunning burst of light that day.

When we arrived at the surgical center, Brian put on a good show, making the women checking us in laugh. They guided me to one door and him to another, the first of many departures that day. A few minutes later, he came back to me while I was getting my IV situated and being swabbed for COVID.

"Finally, a negative test after all these years," I said, smiling, desperate for some lightness. After that, Brian was allowed to sit with me for several hours while I waited to be taken back. The woman before me was running over, and nurses kept pulling back my curtain to apologize for my wait.

I felt sick at the thought of a woman waking up to worse news than she expected. We didn't turn on the television while we waited. Mostly, we sat in the quiet. What is there to say to someone who has done this with you before? Who sits through your colonoscopies every year? Who must feel like a helpless bystander? I told him thank you several times, and each time, Brian shook his head. He didn't want to be thanked. His part was easy.

I imagined spinning the threads of my molecular code into a scarf or a shawl, something warm and protective that would show Ben and Andy that a risk of cancer is not a death sentence. If they inherited my mutation, I needed them to see it as an inconvenient matter of course as they continued living their lives, not something to become obsessed with or paralyzed by. But to do this, I needed to eradicate my own fears first. I could show them how to live with Lynch syndrome only by doing it myself.

Eventually, it was time for me to go back. I said goodbye to Brian for the final time that day. As they wheeled me down a seemingly endless hallway toward the operating chamber, I felt warm tears on my cheeks. I was glad for the mask that covered most of my face. Each time I was separated from Brian and alone with myself that day, I cried. Quiet tears draining me of nameless emotions, needing release.

My ice-cold operating room was a white cavern filled with screens and equipment and so many people. Each one introduced themselves and told me what they would be doing. I appreciated their humanity. Dr. McGinnis came in last and rested his hand on my shoulder as the anesthesiologists injected medicine into my IV. This warm hand on my shoulder was such an unexpected kindness and the last thing I remembered before waking up.

When Brian walked into my recovery space, I'd never been happier to see him in my life. In my post-anesthesia haze, his entire presence radiated love toward me. He placed his hands on my cheeks. "Everything went perfectly," he said, before kissing my forehead.

The roads were thick with snow as we drove back home across Cleveland that evening. I was loopy and sore, but on the other side of surgery, so I perched in my seat and watched the snowflakes swirl. For the second time that day, I put my full trust in someone else to take care of everything.

As we drove through the flurries swirling like a vortex, Brian's fingers gripped the steering wheel. We'd been gone thirteen hours at this point, and he'd been awake through all of them. "Your doctor said something to me, right afterwards, when you were still in the first recovery room."

"I was in two rooms?" I only remembered one.

He nodded, still staring straight ahead. "He said I had to pay attention to you and to make you call him if you don't seem like yourself. He told me you wouldn't notice if your hormones weren't working right, but I probably would." He reached one hand toward the top of my thigh and rested it there for a few blocks. This was exactly what I'd been afraid of. It seemed like one more thing I had to accept that was beyond my control, and I wondered if that feeling would ever go away.

I watched the snowflakes, fluttering against the streetlights, illuminated for a second before floating sideways through the air. I heard Brian's voice. I understood what it said, but I wasn't able to respond aside from tapping the top of his hand three times. Our secret code, one tap for each syllable in *I love you.*

Brian told me to wait in the car while he shoveled the walkway into our house. I leaned against him all the way upstairs to our bed, with Ben and Andy right behind us. I don't remember much else about that night, aside from the enchiladas my dad and his wife dropped off for us being the best food I'd ever eaten. The boys lay with me until they went to bed, and having them close felt healing.

After the boys were in their rooms, my mother-in-law put on my first estrogen patch, her fingers so gentle against the skin of my lower back. There were some conflicting opinions between my surgeon and the women's health specialist, but they agreed I was low risk enough for blood clots that I could begin the patch immediately. I was tired, but felt the adrenaline of having completed a long race.

On the day after surgery, my pain was so acute that I stared at the ceiling or the wall, willing the seconds to pass. In addition to a bottle of acetaminophen, I was given exactly four narcotic painkillers. I was terrified of taking the last one, for fear the pain to come would be too intense to bear and I'd need it later. Though I was desperate for sleep, it was impossible to steal more than a few scraps throughout the day and night.

For the first several days, walking up and down our stairs made me winded. I was only comfortable sitting straight up and down. I was too tired and sore to read or even watch television. When I lifted my shirt in front of the mirror to inspect my incisions, I was shocked by the deep purple bruising on my bloated stomach. My reflection looked like a Georgia O'Keeffe landscape mimicking the female reproductive system.

My plan was to recover while the boys were at school, knowing they were living their lives as usual. I stared out the window at the blanket of whiteness covering my street, unable to do anything else, and it seemed so naive to think I could compartmentalize the hours in the day I'd be healing from the hours I'd be mothering, as if my body were a switch that could flip from one mode to another. But my boys were older now and no longer only taking from me. They fetched me drinks and snacks and gave me the space and time to simply be where I was. They also cared about and worried about me, making them even sweeter.

While sitting upright on the couch or lying completely flat on my bed, I considered how much worse this would be if I was also waiting for pathology reports that would determine my next phase of treatment, if this was a beginning and not an end. I never took the fourth painkiller.

If the first week was harder than I expected, the weeks that followed were all better than anticipated. After two weeks, I took walks every day. I craved the frigid air off Lake Erie in my lungs and the sounds of geese in my ears. I saw leaves waiting to burst from naked trees and watched sunrises and sunsets. One day, I lay on a flat rock next to the frozen lake and felt the sunshine on my face. I spent my days taking walks, reading, writing, and doing the gentlest yoga.

Four weeks after surgery, I had an in-person follow-up with Dr. McGinnis. My incisions had healed beautifully, and the bruising faded to pastel greens and yellows. I didn't have night sweats or hot flashes, indicating that my patch was working, even if I wasn't thrilled with its adhesive qualities. He had put his hand on my shoulder before cutting me open. I wanted to send him a letter during my recovery, an attempt to express my gratitude, but I was unable to focus, and words were infinitesimal compared to the fresh enormity of the feelings brewing inside me anyway.

I was upbeat, and he cleared me for normal living. "Does that mean I'm graduating from you?"

"It's up to you," he answered, before explaining the ongoing annual benefits of gynecological exams and noting that he would be happy to keep seeing me, or I could be seen by Dr. Turner. "It's good we took them now, though," he said. "Your ovaries weren't completely normal." The room constricted around me. My breath tightened within my chest.

He continued. "Pathology showed the beginning of some growths that would have given you trouble in a few years."

They were not cancerous or even precancerous, but the unsaid word ringing in my ears was "yet."

In the elevator, I texted Brian: All clear. Love you. I wasn't lying. This was the bottom line. The truth. I was clear. My ovaries had been sliced and mounted on microscope slides, their secrets laid bare under the gaze of well-trained pathologists. They were imperfect, but they were gone. This was exactly why I'd pursued genetic testing in the first place.

Surgery was my preventive medicine. Intellectually, I understood this. But as I walked out of the cancer center, past the blurry faces of people who I envisioned would have killed for the chance to remove their precancerous organs early, I felt something else. Gurgling rage swelled up in my stomach, pushing against my spine and into my pelvis. An animal with a heartbeat of its own, awakening.

What I wanted, after all these years, was to be told it had all been a mistake. That my mismatch repair genes were doing their jobs, that I was keeping them healthy and functional, that I was normal, that this was all erring on the side of extreme precaution.

In the parking garage, the helplessness hit me like it had the day I learned my brother needed his colon removed. I paid my fare and couldn't wait to be free from the garage and from the entire hospital. As soon as I was back outside, the tears came. I pounded on my steering wheel at a red light. I knew I should be grateful, but I was unable to stoke a drop of gratitude to life.

When I walked in the door, Brian knew something was amiss. As I told him my ovaries would have needed to come out anyway a couple of years down the road, his eyes narrowed. Then he turned away.

"Thank you," I said, "for feeling the way I'm feeling." I needed every shred of his validation.

"I guess this is why you did it, right?" He exhaled, a submission to these facts that never stopped feeling overwhelming.

~

A few days later, I had Ben in the car, on our way home from basketball practice. He was taller than I was and had been for close to a year, his transition from child to adult fully underway. He picked up the empty prescription box I had taken to the doctor from the console. "What's this?"

"It's the box for my patch that I took to show the doctor." I did my best to hide my self-consciousness.

"You have a patch?" He asked like it was scandalous. I was curious how he knew about medicine patches and what worried him about them, but I forced myself to stay focused on the questions at hand.

I nodded and he continued. "For how long?"

"About twenty years or so." The church steeple I'd prayed to twenty-nine years earlier stood watch in the distance, and snowflakes peppered the windshield like white spiders before dissolving.

"You have to wear a patch for the *rest of your life*? Don't you think you should have told me that?"

We'd been having lots of conversations about puberty over the last year, but my body and menopause—or as I pictured it, the opposite of puberty—had never been the subject of these discussions. I felt so insecure about my own body that it made me sorry for the public nature of the chemical reactions taking place in his. "I wasn't sure this was something you wanted to know," I said.

"Of course I want to know these things. God, Mom, I don't understand you sometimes."

He wanted to know.

He wanted to know me.

When we were home later, I asked him if he wanted to see it. When I said "it," he knew exactly what I was talking about. Andy was doing pull-ups in his doorway, and since he hates to be left out of anything, he came into the bathroom too. My patch sat on the low part of my back, rotating which butt cheek it grazed each week, so I had to raise my shirt and tug down my yoga pants a tiny bit.

"I was curious about what that was," Andy said. They were shooting hoops in Ben's room a minute later, but there it was, again: the relief of being seen.

SUMMER 2022

Off-Balance

I was still working from home that summer, amid the chaotic freedom of the kids' vacation. Andy interrupted my virtual meetings, and Ben never stopped asking for food. My office still hadn't reopened for in-person work. We had an influx of funding to plan outdoor spaces, programs, and art projects in the postpandemic landscape. In spite of this, I still did most of my work from the sunroom on our second floor, a room that had formerly been a quiet, peaceful space filled with plants and books.

There were no longer any boundaries around anything in my life. I'd been promoted over the years, and now instead of working with artists and designers, I managed the staff who worked with artists and maintained the relationships with our clients. I spent seemingly every waking moment trying, and failing, to keep everyone on both ends of my computer happy. To keep our projects moving forward, to keep my children from becoming feral brain-dead jerks, to keep my marriage fulfilling.

Instead, I disliked everyone on both sides of my screen—especially, it seemed, the face I stared at all day, every day, trapped in my office, my life, and my body.

"You need to get them out of this house!" I yelled down the stairway to Brian, who was listening to a podcast about UFOs on the couch with a fan blowing on his face.

"I thought we could do something all together once you were done for the day," he said, calling up from the bottom of the stairs.

"I'm never going to finish if I can't have some uninterrupted time to actually do my job." Frustration radiated up and down my limbs.

Before the pandemic, they spent summer vacations having Charkosky Boys Summer Camp, which basically meant they did whatever they wanted all day long while I worked at my office. This was the third summer in a row, however, that I witnessed what I perceived as their extreme laziness. Brian took the boys to various sports camps and other activities, but for the most part, they lounged, ate, scrolled, and bickered. Meanwhile, I moved through a relentless churn of virtual meeting rooms, forcing myself to switch gears every thirty to sixty minutes without any changes in scenery.

Brian packed the boys up with their baseball gear and took them to the batting cages. I ate a bowl of cereal in blissful silence, feeling guilty for my outburst. When they returned, they left their helmets and mitts and bats in the walkway between the kitchen and the back door. I stubbed my toe on a bat.

"Goddammit!" I shrieked, and bent over to inspect my foot. "What is wrong with you guys?"

"You okay, Mama?" Andy asked, kneeling beside me.

Ben rolled his eyes and shook his head at Andy. "Dude, why is Mom always like this now?"

"Like what? You guys have literally everything, and you fight about it all day long." I stomped up the stairs as loud as possible and slammed the door to my office. Summer needed to end. My family's so-called break was breaking me.

I stared at my computer, fuming. I heard a knock on the door, and Brian came in before I answered.

"What?" I asked.

"Tiff, we need to talk."

"About what? About how you need to actually do things with our kids every day?"

"Oh, okay." He nodded. "I see where this is going." He had a smirk when he was angry, like a lying smile. It always enraged me.

I pointed to my laptop. "Can't you see I'm trying to work here?"

"I'm done with this. You need to call your doctor."

"You need to see a therapist or get a hobby."

"I'm serious." Brian turned toward the window, overlooking our street below. "He said you wouldn't know when you needed help."

I shook my head. This wasn't happening.

"This isn't who you are," he said. "It's been going on for months."

"I need you to leave."

Brian walked out. I heard the door to our bedroom close. I didn't remember what I used to feel like or how I used to be. Everything felt hard. Between the grind of my kids getting older, challenging projects and fundraising goals at work, and not knowing if or when we'd return to an office, there were more than enough external factors for me to blame my internal turmoil on. Brian questioning my medications made me feel like a hysterical woman, unable to have any sort of feelings about the world without her sanity being called into question.

But, a few months earlier, I'd switched from a hormone patch I changed once a week to a twice-weekly one. The first patch was large and bubbled on my skin. It left my flesh raw and irritated. The new patch I was on was much smaller, with a gentler adhesive. As I considered whether my current distaste for everyone I loved was a chemical problem, heat spread through my body in a wave of painful humiliation.

I stared at my hands, freckled and veiny, and chewed on my lip until I tasted blood. Brian and I had been arguing all summer, and most of the time it was because he was doing something wrong. But what if I was at least partially wrong? I sat with this question for a long time before dialing the number to the women's health specialist, ashamed of what I would have to say to the voice that answered on the other end. Afraid that there was nothing they could do to help.

~

A week later, Dr. Turner wrinkled her nose as she reviewed my most recent round of blood work with me. "I don't like these numbers at all," she said, squinting at her computer screen. "I'm not sure what happened here. This dosage is what we prescribe to people who still have their ovaries and just need a little boost." It turned out that when my patch changed, the estrogen dosage was cut in half.

"My husband told me I haven't been acting like myself," I said. "And when I thought about it, I guess I realized I haven't really been feeling like myself either." My voice caught in my throat. "Being mean to my family was the exact thing I was afraid of."

She clicked back and forth between different parts of my chart. "Well, it hasn't been so long that your bones would have weakened, but I'm pretty upset about this. You should have had months of feeling a lot better than you have. I'm going to double the estrogen dose and add testosterone." She rattled off the slew of vitamins I should be taking and suggested a follow-up blood test in a month.

When I saw Brian later that day, I burst into tears. "I'm so sorry," I said, leaning into him and rubbing my forehead against his chest. He smelled like the grass he'd just cut.

"This is good, though, right? Having answers." He cupped his hand around the back of my head. "Did you know, before I said something?"

I squeezed my eyes shut against him and shook my head. "How can I trust my own feelings anymore?"

"You'll have to trust us."

This seemed impossible for me to imagine for the rest of my life. At the same time, it felt like the race we'd been training our whole relationship for. Nobody in the world knew me and loved me the way Brian did. But I'd have to do my part too and share when things seemed overwhelming or out of control. I had no choice but to dial in and listen to myself and be unafraid to ask for help.

Brian's face was tan from the summer sun, and his beard had grown out. He called it "summer hippie," and instead of being jealous of his break, I was happy to have him home. I hadn't even started my new medications yet, but having this information, painful as it was, made me strong enough to see everything around me more clearly. I loved the worn copper-penny color of Brian's eyes and the way I knew exactly how to rest my head against him. "Thank you for loving me enough to tell me these things," I said, loving that he always did the right thing, even when it was hard.

SUMMER 2022

Let Go

A few weeks later, right before school started, I took the boys to an indoor climbing park, one of Andy's happy places. It had a couple different ropes courses, a zip line, walls to climb, and several obstacles to maneuver through. Originally, I only intended to watch the boys, but after a while it looked too fun to just observe from the sidelines. The teenage worker buckled me into a harness and showed me how to clip and unclip the metal fasteners.

When Andy and Ben saw me suited up, they cheered, "Let's go!" like I was one of their buddies, a friend with strict parents who was finally allowed freedom.

We climbed a stack of enormous Rubik's Cubes. Each square was at a different angle, and I needed to concentrate on where to put my fingers and how to position my feet as I climbed. I felt my heart pounding and wondered if I'd overdone it, if my internal stitches would rupture. As I clawed my way up like Spider-Man, Andy was already cascading to the bottom. Feeling his eyes on me from the ground was motivating. I didn't want him to see me give up. My fingers gripped the cube, and I pushed my thigh up and over the edge into a new position.

I kept going, one breath, one movement, at a time. Reaching the top, I felt the same pure triumph I'd experienced when I ran my first three miles without stopping. But then I made the mistake of turning to look back toward Andy, who waved up to me with a huge gap-toothed smile. Ben landed next to him a moment later.

They both looked so far away.

Andy cupped his hands around his mouth and yelled, "Mom, just lean back and let go! You won't fall, I promise!"

If we ever lived through a natural disaster and they were about to be swallowed by the earth, I'd have to be brave. Being brave looked different every day. Some days it was facing my medical team and hoping for another all clear. Some days it was being the mother I wish I'd had, playing with my boys or making them try things they'd avoid without the push. Most days it has become waking up before dawn to dump these swirling thoughts onto paper and into some kind of order I could make sense of.

Today, it was climbing to the top of a house-size Rubik's Cube and trusting that once I let go, I wouldn't smash into the ground. With my heart drumming inside my ears, I tugged on the vest and buckles with my free hand, thinking about what the past decade had entailed: climbing, pushing, trusting, knowing when to keep going and when to let go.

I took a deep breath, closed my eyes, and pushed off from the towering wall, while an invisible orchestra thrummed inside me. Lights shone all around, but I had an audience of only two. My boys' applause became the soundtrack to this moment as I floated backward, weightless, suspended in midair.

And then I saw them, standing below, ready to catch me before my feet hit the ground.

SUMMER 2024

Today

Andy's white pin-striped baseball uniform is covered in dust. His neck and arms are tan and without freckles. There's only a cinnamon sprinkle across his nose. His eyes are bright blue, exactly the same as his Grandma Suzie's and Uncle Sam's. He'd tried out for a super-competitive baseball club last autumn, and we spent all winter and spring driving him to his practices in the next county.

He's about to turn twelve. He's a lefty. He looks like my dad.

My miracle baby, the one I worried I'd never have, grabs his mitt and sprints to left field. He's still small, with his young voice, months or more away from starting his growth spurt. He catches my eyes and gives me a thumbs-up.

Ben follows Andy with a digital camera. He's become the tallest person in our house, a lanky replica of Brian's grandfather who lived into his nineties. I love seeing the different traits of our relatives coming back to life in new configurations, of watching these biological secrets unfold with time. Ben and his pack of friends ride their bikes around Lakewood and have played baseball together for the past eight seasons. He'll go home later and edit his footage into a video he'll set to music. I'll catch him deep inside a world he's created, turning life into art.

He's just finishing his first year of high school. Earlier this week, he told me that Lynch syndrome came up in his English class. "Isn't that what you have?" he asked. After I confirmed it was, he continued. "You know there's a girl in my class whose grandma also died from Lynch syndrome? Her mom has it too." He'd pulled open the pantry and rummaged for a snack. "Didn't you write something about Lynch syndrome? I want to show her." He's so unscarred, so unashamed, so unguarded. I know Ben's life will bring its own setbacks, but being here to help him navigate these years is a gift I feel with every cell, every day.

It wouldn't matter if I had one more day with them, or a century. It will never be enough time. I still have so much to teach them, so much to learn from them. How would anyone ever be able to say goodbye?

I'd packed a cooler when the house was still quiet, filled with fruit and other healthy snacks that will be shunned in favor of concession-stand fare, but I can't help myself. I forced everyone to wear sunscreen, even though I'm the only one who burns.

I'm here in the bleachers with the sun on my face because at the end of his life, my uncle agreed to have a conversation with a stranger who studied genetics. He imagined a different future for his sister's family, for the buds on branches of his family tree he'd never meet. I'm twelve years older than my mom ever became, and the exact age that most ovarian cancers are found in women with Lynch syndrome. Last summer, I had another adenoma removed from my colon. I still hate that there was anything to remove at all, but now I accept this knowledge as a fact of my life. So, when my blond almost-twelve-year-old son gets to run onto the baseball field, when his worries are of the banal scholastic or athletic variety, I get the satisfaction of knowing I'm doing my part.

There were no letters from my mother. No tiny notes scribbled on scraps and tucked into our drawers to be found later. But there are the quilts and the cross-stitches. There's the knowledge that she gave the fight for her life every drop she had. I feel her with me, eternally inside me, like a conscience or love itself.

~

I woke early this morning to write before the sun rose. Years earlier, I'd started to feel the tiny whisper of thoughts and feelings I needed to explore, like I was resurrecting a younger version of myself. Now, every day I brew coffee and watch the sun brighten the sky out my eastern window. Motherhood has given me a lot of things, but it will never make sure I give my ideas time and attention. I carve this time out of my day, pulling myself from sleep. I'm the mother I wanted, the wife and life partner I aspire to be, the person I've always been when I gift myself this creative time. As much as I wish my DNA was perfect, my mutation is also a permission slip, pushing me closer every day to the best life I can live.

My best life requires finding words for the feelings agitating below my skin. It needs laughter and sunshine, movement and time outside, books, music, art, and the space to try these things myself. I need to show my boys not only how to fight disease, but how to cultivate a life that brings joy. I see beauty all around me, everywhere, all the time.

I see it in the perfectly drawn white chalk lines in the baseball field, in the way the dust puffs up when the players jog through the infield, and hear it in the other parents chatting all around me. A younger version of me would have assumed they all have flawless lives, but now I know they're also carrying stories and heartaches and hopes invisible to me, just as I am to them.

I see it in Brian, who stands behind the chain-link backstop, arms crossed over his chest and eyes on the field, missing nothing. I can't believe I get to build my life with him, that our lives intersected in the smallest of ways years before we ever met, and now we're here with the humans we made, doing what they love. This is a normal day on a normal weekend. But there will never be anything boring or tedious about any of this.

Even if I'm tired from the driving and annoyed about keeping the white baseball pants moderately clean, and even when Andy's in a batting slump or Ben makes two errors in a row or we get home late on a Sunday night to an empty refrigerator and mountains of laundry, I don't take any of it for granted. I don't wish away a single minute.

Instead, I think back to those early days with Brian, when everything we have now seemed like a dream. This is a love letter. Today we're here, in the sun, with our boys. The only path to these ordinary days was the one that led here.

ACKNOWLEDGMENTS

This book exists because my agent, Laurie Dennison, advocated for this story and believed in it from the beginning. Selena James, Ronit Wagman, and the dedicated team at Little A transformed my vision into something even stronger than I ever imagined.

The following people gave this project encouragement and feedback at critical moments throughout its development: Melissa Cleckner, Meghan Cliffel, Jan Godbey, Vivian Harakas, Molly Kimball, Sonja Kreps, Shelley Mann Hite, Deanna Palermo, Amanda Peck, Danielle Rini Uva, Bryony Romer, Sarah Siebert, Jamie Smialek, Jill Smialek, Nancy Sotka, Meg Thompson, and Tessa Zilla.

I have an incredible team of current and past caregivers whose professionalism and compassion are unrivaled, including Dr. Carol Burke, Dr. Robert DeBernardo, Dr. Holly Thacker, Dr. Georgia Wiesner, and Duane Culler, LISW.

Thank you to the small and mighty team at Literary Cleveland for cultivating such a warm, inspiring community of writers. You're making dreams come true.

To my family, who continue to walk every step of this journey with me, thank you for a lifetime of love, care, and guidance.

To Ben and Andy, you make everything I do worth doing.

To Brian, your love and support have sustained me through the highs and lows of life. There's no truer two.

DISCUSSION GUIDE

1. This is a book about grief, love, and how they are intertwined. One of the author's life conundrums is that if she hadn't lost her mother, she wouldn't have the family she has now. Can you think of an event in your life that was cataclysmic but ultimately led you down a path that, in hindsight, you're grateful for?
2. Science and medicine have given us so much information about our physical and mental health. Reflecting on your own family, are there diseases or conditions that influenced them but didn't yet have a name or a more common understanding at the time? What insights does this hindsight offer?
3. Have you considered genetic testing for yourself? What decisions have you made? What would you be afraid to discover? What would you be relieved to learn?
4. If you have children, how much of your medical history do you share with them? How do they respond?
5. Have you ever faced something outside your control? What did you learn about yourself?
6. The author made a series of decisions: to pursue genetic testing, to stop building her family, to have a hysterectomy, to have an oophorectomy, to take hormone replacement. Where would you have made

the same choice for yourself? Where would you have differed?

7. What parts of your childhood have stuck with you as you've grown? Do you have any specific memories that feel particularly formative?
8. Do you remember the moment your childhood ended? Or the moment you felt like a full-fledged adult?
9. What parts of this story feel most hopeful to you? What do you think you'll remember most?

ABOUT THE AUTHOR

Photo © 2025 Kim Wasielewski Photography

Tiffany Graham Charkosky's writing explores love, human dynamics, and relationships. Her essays and short stories have been published in *Gordon Square Review*, *Mutha Magazine*, *The Avalon Literary Review*, and *South Dakota Review*. She lives in Northeast Ohio with her family and has worked in the arts for over twenty years. For more information, visit www.tiffanygrahamcharkosky.com.